THE BOY WITH SHOES

A Kenyan Childhood

HILLARY LISIMBA AMBANI

MYSTERY BOOKS

The Boy with Shoes!

Copyright ©Hillary Lisimba Ambani, 2019

The right by Hillary Lisimba Ambani to be identified as the author of this work has been asserted in accordance with the international copyright laws and Copyright Act Cap. 130 laws of Kenya.

All rights reserved.

ISBN-13: 978-9966-804-91-4

Published by:

Mystery Publishers Limited
P.O. Box 18016 – Nakuru, Kenya
Tel: +254 718 429 184
Email: publishing@mysterypublisherslimited.com
Website: www.mysterypublisherslimited.com

Cover Design by Herbert Manula, ©Mystery Books

Typeset in Garamond 12pt by Mystery Publishers

Printed in the United States of America by CreateSpace, an Amazon.com Company

For

The late Jumba Mamesa

You made English beautiful, effortlessly
I didn't just learn, I experienced
I found love in English, and English opened its arms to me
Sad you never got to see my writing come alive
You should have waited a little bit longer to see me make you
proud.

To your grave, you took a lot of wisdom and language
I try, very hard, to keep your legacy alive,
I hope one day I can make a language champion too
Some say the little things I write inspire them—I don't know
I just write!

They never showed me where your bones lie, nor let me bring
you flowers.
You, too, didn't bid me farewell, you just left—
And that was cruel of you.
Well, I doubt anyone knew just how much you flowed in my
blood.
Heroes don't die,
They forever remain engraved on the hearts of those they
touched.

Tears poured freely as I wrote this poem, I still mourn my English champion.
This book is my little way of saying 'Thank You'.
It's the much I could do.
Now you can rest in peace,
Your legacy lies herein.

Signed,
Son of Man.
Born to tell stories to touch lives.

Also for:

Those who made this possible:

My parents, Mr and Mrs Ambani, for the fists of steel. I was naughty and that is why this book exists in the first place. You also made sure I got sufficient education to help me fit into the modern day society.

Tope, Anthony, Anne, Nelly (Rest in peace), and Julliet. You were the gears in the system that interwove to create this entire plot.

My high school English teacher, Mr. George Masinde, for picking the language orphan left by Mr. Mamesa and crafting me into the prose writer I have become. I owe you another book.

Mr Erick Livumbazi Ngoda, my editor, for helping me re-arrange my ideas into something sensible.

Brenda Oloo (Mermaid): The dotting wife, mother to my son and anchor in my adult years. You took over parenting me from my parents and you've done an excellent job.

Milan: In him my heir lies. In his veins my blood flows. In his existence, I have reason to look forward to another day. Now that is the next writer.

My fans: You are the reason I write. I became your servant and it's a wonderful place to be. For you I'll always write.

Lydiah N. Njuguna, Patricia L. George, and Cassandra Mathews: wonderful strangers who believed in a young man's dream and turned it into a reality. Words aren't sufficient to express my gratitude.

God: That would need a whole book to talk about. He is everything I needed and more.

CONTENTS

PREFACE

This is a true reminiscence, a recollection of my formative years growing up in the village. I have come to realize that it was a rich experience that taught me many valuable life lessons. Although some still make me cry and others make me light up with joy, all the memories are dear and deep inside my heart. They are all indelibly etched in the sands of time. Most people who grew up around the time I did would relate and empathize, because it seemed like every parent during our time read from the same script, every school operated the same way, and every village had the same characters. Some of these stories could sound fictitious to those growing up in the present day but they will definitely strike a nostalgic cord in those with similar experiences.

Hillary Lisimba Ambani, 2019

CHAPTER 1

AN IMBECILE IS BORN

NEWLY MARRIED TO a young man who had put her up in one of the most beautiful houses in the village, Mom's life grew from strength to strength. Her job as a teacher won her love from church members, parents to the children she taught, fellow workmates, and ordinary villagers. A woman, like her, who made her 'own money' in the '90s earned a place among the 'who is who' in the society. The norm was most women stayed home and waited for the men to toil and bring the bacon home. Wait, let us replace 'bacon' with something cheaper, like beans. Most men who went out not only came home smelling of cheap liquor, but also demanded food from the same women they had left with no money. I lost count of the fathers I passed lying on the roadside after one too many, waiting for their lovely wives to come drag their drunk souls home.

It is, therefore, safe to say that Mom was living the Kenyan Dream … but there was a problem: the only son she had given birth to was the proper definition of an imbecile. She named me after one of the most famous doctors of our time, Dr Lisimba. The only undoing was that my surname is Luhyia for Mongoose, doctor in the picture or not. For the same reason, the name 'Lisimba' was not fully embraced by the family, because families share surnames passed on from generation to generation. All my sisters have some other cousin or a niece with their maiden names as Savai, Afandi, Eboso, or some other family name. The names keep circulating as new babies join our family, so much that many a time when we are at a gathering you have to specify 'the small Savai' or 'the chubby Eboso' lest six people respond at the same time. It is only that these gatherings are rare these days—we forgot family ties and only meet at funerals.

Back to my name, Lisimba has never been given to anyone else, it is like the whole extended family silently protested against it. Even my own four-year-old son has internalized all my other names but somehow refused to grasp this particular one. That is what happens when you go naming your kid after tiny crafty stubborn animals just because you picked the name from a doctor.

I choose not to take this lying down, though. Remove 'Li' from the same name and you are left with 'Simba', the king of the jungle. Now that makes sense, doesn't it? Dogs named Simba in my village not only have a personality but are known to be fierce. So, if some comfort can be gained from that then I left that mongoose crap and joined the winning side; and that's how early in life 'The Den Diaries' was born. Lions have dens, mongoose have holes; the lion roars and everything around goes into hiding, the mongoose hears simple noises and scampers into hiding. Who in their right mind wants to be associated with that kind of mediocrity? Not me. The LION it is.

I have never been told the exact time of the day that I came, kicking and screaming, into this world. Only the date is deemed important to record perhaps, mine being Friday, 10th May, 1985. The location of birth is recorded as Pumwani Maternity Hospital, the largest maternity facility in Kenya. Further details surrounding my entry into the world are scanty, but I have with time come to question a lot of things. First, that facility has had numerous scandals of babies being exchanged when their mothers are still confused and weak from labour. Which means I could easily be a child of affluence who should by now be sitting in a rocking chair in a compound with an Olympic-size swimming pool sipping mojito to the sound of birds chirping on trees.

However, I live in a lower middle class apartment jostling for space with giant cockroaches during the day and giant mosquitoes at night. I always confirm my jalopy has working jumper cables and a tow-rope in the trunk before leaving lest it 'dies' on me out there. Being broke is just sad, isn't it? Secondly, I'm constantly confused with an artist named Rabbit (shares this love for animals). He is into creative writing with a similar style as mine and is Luhyia like myself! Coincidence? Who knows, one of these days I'll drag myself to a lab and run DNA tests.

I am the first born, an only son, which automatically meant I was a mini-parent. My parents didn't have much back then; just two huts, a handful of brown chicken, one emaciated cow, and God. When you are born of a family that is still trying to find a bearing, you suffer together with your parents, and when their little money runs out, they look at you with such thoughts as, 'if we didn't have this third mouth, we would probably have some more.' They also make all their parenting mistakes on you and the society understands. Even as a trial and error kid, a guinea-pig, you are expected to be as straight as an arrow, as if someone tapped you one day while in the womb and said he was there for a crash course on discipline. You become some sort of a magician's dove; raised a mistake, turned out a masterpiece.

Mothers usually bear the brunt, because fathers easily conclude your wailing into one sentence—he wants to breastfeed—and only one person in that household has that ability. Sometimes one wonders why men were given this useless pair on the chest, but then imagine a man's chest without breasts. When you do well at school, the father guards that victory as his own, when you fail the same father avoids it like the plague— *wewe tu ni mjinga kama mamako.*

First-born sons gave fathers pride and agony in equal measure. Pride because they went to work and their first result was a male made them feel like a bull. It brought about an air of importance knowing there's a ready heir to continue the family lineage and inherit their property. Well, it is not like most had anything to call an inheritance, maybe just debts for those that spent their twilight years drowning in illicit liquor. The agony was that sons were darlings to their mothers—some sort of connection even scientists haven't done well at explaining—so, fathers hang on and sometimes throw tantrums to remain relevant. The weak ones kept distance, pretending to be out there working when they actually were tired of how upside down another little being turned their cul-de-sac.

First-borns can easily break young marriages, because a once active sex life metamorphoses into a cot of cries and poop. The couple walk around with red sleepy eyes from lack of sleep, many times fighting over who should clear the poop or feed the baby at night. Sex dry spells hit an all-time high because the baby 'refuses' to move from the matrimonial bed to the crib. Mothers side with their 'angel', allowing the baby to sleep spread-eagle between them. One minute the baby is on top of the new parents' heads, the next minute is threatening to drop from the bed to the ground, then the two have to put up with another round of wailing, kicking, and whimpering.

Ever been a father and wanted to say 'son of a gun' then remembered the gun in question was you? By morning, the young wife-cum-mother-of-your-child keeps talking about breastfeeding, washing the baby, getting millet flour for the baby, immunizations that are due for the baby … now add an imbecile like me to the equation and suicide hovered around like a debt collector.

Growing up and schooling in the village was mayhem. First, you were weaned on cow milk and porridge, then raised in napkins which had to be washed over and over at the rate you soiled them, and a baby that's being weaned poops things that are unprintable. Add first-born to that list and you were doomed from the word go. If my example is anything to go by, first-born kids are also born specifically for punishment. I was more than once blamed for the mistakes of my younger siblings; half the time being whipped on their behalf. For some reason, African parents are slap-happy. By the time they are threatening to punish a mistake you are already juggling between holding onto balance and rubbing off the pain on the cheeks courtesy of slaps you did not manage to count.

First-born sons, however, do not look at their mother straight in the eye and challenge whatever she says, however idiotic it is. Most mothers would be quick to remind you that they breastfed and wiped your ass so you have no right of expression. Wasn't breastfeeding and cleaning poop a rider when they made their decision to bring a baby into the world?

It was a crime to try to block those slaps. It was considered a murder plot against your mother.

"Ati umefanya nini? Heeeee, unataka kuniua sasa, sindio?"

That simple act of saving yourself some pain would be repeated everywhere whenever people spoke of bad children. If someone praised you on the road for being well mannered, your mom would interject:

"Nooo. Polite? Let him not pretend here, this one almost killed me the other day!"

That was mom, always tagging along a little would-be murderer and reminding villagers that I may not be armed but was very dangerous. A child who blocked the parent's slaps was a threat to society, everyone had to be wary.

Dad worked in Nairobi and visited once a month, most probably the day his salary reflected on the account. He loved traveling at night, so we would go to bed as usual on Friday evening and wake up to an additional member the following morning. You did not have to struggle much to know he was around even as he snored the night's journey away. Mom was up and down around the house fixing meals with more vigour than we were used to.

The realisation came as bad news; that all the unpunished mistakes throughout the month would be read out and punished at supper time. Dad would wake up and start barking orders at everyone, like a hungry lion traversing the jungle. His hoarse voice sent shivers down everyone, including the farm workers and Bobby the family dog. His being away was in a way a blessing to us, but then again it deprived us of the paternal love we needed at that developmental stage. It created a long-term relationship breakdown that we have to this day not fully recovered from.

Nestling in the quiet land of Maragoli is Chotero village, the place I call home. Although it is considered an agricultural zone, girls are more fertile than the farms. During the planting season, the villagers woke up early every morning to drop maize and bean seeds into holes sunk in the ground the previous day. The lazy one was usually asked to go to the farm a little later, his or her role being to cover up the holes with soil. After that much toiling, the farms produced maize cobs the size of a home theatre remote control. It was like the land of my birth badly needed to break away from some generational curse, otherwise the mathematics of planting crops, waiting for three months then eating the harvest in two weeks did not sit well with me.

Where we lacked in fertility, Chotero enjoyed the abundance of circular grass-thatched mud huts with a long pole protruding at the peak. It was like those little umbrella-like structures came with lightning arresters. The rich few roofed their houses with iron sheets, mostly done way before I was born because by the time I was mature enough, they were all brown and rusty, evidence of how much the weather had beaten them. When boys came of age, they were advised to start life in a grass-thatched house, then upgrade with time to iron sheets roofs.

But the years moved so fast that before one knew it, what was meant to be a temporary structure had become his family house and at least three children had been created under it. I am being modest by putting the child-count at three, because my boys fill this earth with wanton disregard for family planning. Consequently, school fees would start choking the poor young man, and the dream to upgrade to an iron-roofed house flew out of the window. Those that were lucky enough to escape the village and land a job in the city had higher chances of building better houses. The problem with those in the city was, however, that most opened their eyes to partying and womanizing, until their bosses slid a termination letter under their desks one morning. The brighter ones would hit the road, find another job and change their lifestyles, investing back home lest the new boss followed in the footsteps of the previous one.

Most grass-thatched houses had four rooms; lounge, bedroom, kitchen, and animal room. In other words, our fowls had a whole room to themselves in the family house. I think whoever came up with the line 'chicken came home to roost' had spent time in my village. Your worth was determined by how big your sitting room was, and whether there was a different part for the dining area. A long cupboard rested against the wall with no window, the more affluent one with see-through glasses from which you could view the household's cutlery and crockery which were only used when visitors came over. All the other days the family made do with rusted cups, torn plates and plastic tumblers as cockroaches roamed through the collection tucked away in wait for an event.

There were three types of cooking points for the kitchen. One was the traditional three stones, the other a slight improvement of the stones called the modern-jiko which operated on chunks of wood instead of firewood, and the proper charcoal *jiko*. This third one was mostly lit on weekends to cook heavy meals like beans, maize, or the mixture. Dangling from the kitchen roof was a stack of firewood, replenished almost daily by the girls who were tasked with fetching dry pieces of wood and tree trunks from around the village. The moneyed bought full trees, chopped into smaller pieces and stashed them on that overhead 'store' to dry from the kitchen heat.

The pit latrine and bathroom were proper green structures in the sense that one 'grew' them with plants that had heavy dark leaves. All one needed was to plant many of them in a circle or square, and after a while a green structure would rise from ground up. The opening meant for the door would be covered with a towel or old blanket, and just like that a construction problem was solved.

Hedges surrounded most compounds, save for one or two who were wealthy enough to afford barbed wire. Gates to these compounds were either next to the main road or facing a footpath that linked to the main road.

A house was proof that a young man was now eligible to move to the neighbouring village and get a girl and find a way to bring her back to our village. But winning a girl in that village was a long tedious process and you would not have gained the courage to approach a girl from elsewhere before honing your skills on those around you. First, no boy approached the said girl alone; just in case she said no. That crop of girls would not say no and leave it at that, they always followed the rejection with a series of loud insults. This left those around in stitches as you tried to muster some energy to take your dejected soul back home.

In such scenarios, go-betweens came in handy. These were the self-proclaimed 'macho' boys who didn't fret about approaching a girl. They knew way too early in time that approaching a girl would only yield two answers; 'No' to mean 'I'm game but just playing hard-to-get' or silence which meant a dead end. They would go to the girl, present your case, convince her on your behalf then arrange a meeting to 'introduce' the two of you. By the time this introduction was done, the girl had been wooed fully and was already yours; you only had to pick from there. Both the boy and girl would be too shy to look into each other's eyes, so the girls would be chewing fingernails or mauling and shredding leaves and tiny branches of the nearest trees and thickets while the boy would be doodling on the ground with his big toe.

The go-between was then promoted to relationship messenger. All mail would go from one party to the other through him or her. This was, however, an expensive affair because the correspondent had to be paid by the boy before offering the services. Payment would include an oval bottle of 'Yu Body Jelly' for a female correspondent and hard cash for a male. However, the bigger budget would go into impressing the girl.

A boy would have done anything possible to get some money, buy a few things and give them to the correspondent. The risk was that most correspondents edited the list of items before delivering them to the intended destination, so chances were that half the package would not get there. Go-betweens were shrewd business people, unless it was one of those cool brothers who didn't mind you dating the sister.

When an assignment like that presented, they would do due diligence on the target then wait in the bushes, camouflaged like leopards, to 'push' (escort) the girl to or from the river. Permission to 'push' was never granted, you imposed yourself and yapped all the things your mind could muster, as she struggled to outpace you, balancing the heavy load on her head. She could give you one-word answers or a forced smile, but that was a sign that she was willing to let you hang around, because a girl that didn't want you only needed to say two words—*"Nitaambia Mamangu"*—and you stopped right in your tracks. A girl reporting that you were talking her into partaking 'bad manners' with you while she tried to be a responsible daughter was tantamount to murder. You were lucky if her father lived and worked in the city, because only the mother would show up at your door that very evening, a *leso* around her waist, stand arms akimbo then hurl insults at you for spoiling children, and your mom for bringing into the world a raunchy goat always on heat.

The well-tamed mothers would be silent and patient, let the other mother finish howling across the neighbourhood and go back to her house, then offer you warm water for a bath. While bathing, as naked as the day you were born, your mother would storm into the bathroom with a pair of slippers or a piece of wood. You wouldn't want to be in the same room with your irate mother, slippers/the cane in hand, you naked, afraid and freezing. Even raising a hand without actually hitting you felt like gunshot, and crying was a felony ... crying meant you looked down upon her punishment. When the slippers didn't seem to administer what she had in store, her fingers kicked in. I still have pinch marks imprinted on my thighs as evidence.

It was a different story if the same information reached the girl's father. They were civilized not to come into another man's compound and spew venom, maybe because they had been worse during their time, or scared that your father might be home and things could get ugly. Men didn't fight on each other's compounds, especially not in front of kids, screaming and jeering and not even when there was a greater risk of going back home with missing teeth, this usually meant your kids quickly became laughing stocks for having a self-inflicted *kibogoyo* father.

Imagine being at a gathering and someone asks, *"Samson, meno ilienda wapi?"*

"Haiya, hujaskia? Alienda kupigana juzi kwa Ambani wakagonga meno. Huyu sasa ni kibogoyo tu."

"Sasa mahindi utakula vipi?"

"Mgani? Mahindi hawezi. Huyu sasa ni wa uji tu."

It was not like they would be saying this behind your back, no, you would be seated with them, mouth shut, not sure whether to say something, laugh along, or feel stupid.

So to mitigate future embarrassments, the girl's father would watch you from a distance, know your routine, then waylay you. Some even made plans with the daughter to accept your 'push' then he would appear from nowhere wielding a machete or a whip and beat the crap out of you. So you would be there, facing imminent death, while the girl you wanted watched and laughed at how her father was tackling a manner-less son of a woman. That is also the reason daughters tend to gravitate towards their fathers, because in them they see protection, real love and the one man who is serious when he promises to be there for her through thick and thin.

Being beaten over a girl was information you had to keep top secret, because if your own parents got wind of it, there would be another session so you dashed to the river, washed your face and limbs to erase any evidence, then waited for the swelling to subside before walking back home a humble young man.

A lot has changed, because would-be agricultural farms have since become settlement land. Some of my folks have (against Luhyia culture) sold ancestral land to people from 'foreign' tribes who are using it for high-rise buildings and private schools. The macho men of our society are adopting new ways of life among them styling hair, piercing ears, and getting down with fellow men. The girls we chased around and got beaten for now chase the boys, and go-betweens have been replaced by a little mobile phone applications like WhatsApp, Telegram, Facebook, and many others who conduct social analytics and recommend girls for you. Fathers have no one to waylay, and the unlucky few who fall victim to thrashing can no longer keep the information to themselves because one screenshot spreads past the village at the click of a forward icon. Mothers no longer go to people's compounds to stand arms akimbo; they are busy meeting at cafés to do table banking and apply for *chama* loans. Village life has become boring.

CHAPTER 2

WELCOME TO SCHOOL

WHEN OUR HOUSE-help decided not to show up for work one morning, Mom tagged me along to the school she taught and dumped me with the nursery school kids while she took on her usual teaching duties. By the time she came to pick me over lunch hour, I was part of the system; too deeply immersed to take a step back. She hurriedly assembled some pencils, drawing books and crayons then crocheted a blue and white shoulder-sling school bag. She now had company every morning to work in the form of a young boy waddling behind her like a duck. Mom and I were now like two peas in a pod, only that the bigger pea understood what was going on, among them the fact that I had helped her put the need for a nanny aside, albeit temporarily.

Mutsulyu Primary School sat at the junction of two roads, one leading to Lyaduywa and the other Mbihi, the way to my home. The lower part of it was hidden by a badly planted hedge with loopholes through which truants made their way out. The gate was just an opening with no structure to give it the name. It was a state of mind, and both teachers and students knew which part was the no man's land and where the school compound started without the demarcation. A signpost with the school name painted on it stood a meter away from the imaginary crossing line, threatening to collapse any time. The writings, though defaced, were precise:

MUTSULYU PRIMARY SCHOOL
P.O. BOX 82, MARAGOLI

No motto, no fancy graffiti, nothing. Such academic arrogance!

The classroom block was an inverted L-shape, with the staffroom holed at the meeting point between the horizontal and vertical axes. The shorter side of the L was lower primary, the longer upper primary—classes four to eight. In front of the classroom was an assembly area, denoted by a tall wooden pole on which the Kenya flag was hoisted every morning Monday and Friday. That flag was more than a symbol of patriotism, as it ushered us back from the weekend and sent us away after a long week of assignments and the cane.

At the Assembly Area, stones were arranged in four concentric circles like a stadium; the smallest circle for class one and two, all the way to class eight on the outside. A student's name would only be mentioned during assembly because he or she either did something exceptionally good or was involved in what would ordinarily pass for simple misdemeanour like making faces at a girl. All the other times it was teachers threatening us with failure, the cane, or being 'chased to bring fees.'

The classrooms were simple halls with wooden windows and floors smeared in either clay or cow dung. They reeked of dust and jiggers. Some were in so bad a shape that water had to be sprinkled on before they were swept. The interior walls were dotted with charts and diagrams on manila papers—hand made by teachers, some not as creative. Eyesore is the word, but we had to put up with them either way. Inside the classes, desks were arranged in three columns, the first column near the door a preserve for the top performers, the middle for the average, and the column at the far side . . . you know who. On the desks sat three students, usually two boys and a girl at the centre or vice versa, an arrangement we hated to high heavens. It was only in our teen years after struggling to approach girls that we realised we should have grabbed those chances with both hands.

Our uniform was a startling ensemble of yellow shirts, a maroon pair of shorts, and maroon pullovers. The shorts were hardly long enough to touch the knees. The girls wore long maroon dresses with shades of yellow on the belt and collar, and green and yellow bloomers for games kits. Half the pullovers in the school were chewed at the edges (not chewed by rats, but by the very same wearers as a pastime) and had elbows protruding out.

My life took off in 1992 when my Mom's youngest brother, Hudson, joined our household while I was joining Class Two. Hudson's second name is Vodohi, Luhyia for 'mud', *'matope'* in Swahili. The first two letters were slashed to leave it at 'Tope', and it worked perfectly. Everyone called him 'Tope'. His introduction brought about two significant changes in my life. First, I now had a best friend, and second, Mom could now shake me off her back. Tope was two years older than I was but, thanks to his small body frame, we easily passed for twins. He was my first real secondary attachment, the one I nurtured social skills on. Forget Bonnie and Clyde, we were inseparable and troublesome.

Tope's class was separated from mine by a wall but no ceiling, so whatever transpired in the other room was heard across loud and clear. With teachers shouting themselves hoarse, we knew who performed well there, who had received a tongue-lashing and who had received a beating for submitting an assignment late. Their terror was their math teacher; Madam Zubeda, who doubled up as the school headmistress. She was light-complexioned, short and plump. She had a penchant for huge handbags and enormous earrings. She spoke with the authority of a court judge, walked like a big bad bully, and had a love affair with the cane—forever meting out justice to Tope and his classmates. Like Mom, she was a harsh. It was impossible for her lesson to end without someone being caned, and for that my class was forced recipient of collateral trauma.

Maths was always taught in the morning, when your mind was still recovering from breakfast and the long walk to school, or the hide and seek you had gone through trying to circumvent the morning routine chores at the school. One of rote prayers was that Madam Zubeda never became my teacher, because maths was not nice to me either on the other side of the wall. On this particular prayer, heavens know why, God was deaf. I have never forgotten that fateful day Madam Zubeda walked into our class clutching a black handbag and announced that she would be teaching us … MATHEMATICS! I almost dropped out of school that very day.

While she lay down the rules of engagement, I sat at my desk rubbing the goose bumps on my trembling thighs. I heard very little of what she said; all I remember was a below-the-knee dress accentuated by large round green earrings that kept swinging from side to side. The horrifying beatings we had hitherto just experienced in the abstract from beyond the wall had come home. Her introductory meeting came to a completion without anyone being punished, but I had been lost in my own world that I failed to hear a critical point.

One of her first orders was that the following day, each one of us was to bring fifty counters—small sticks cut to the same size and used to help in counting during the lesson. The idea was that if you were told to add twelve to thirteen, you would count twelve out of the bunch, then another thirteen, put them together and give the total. That was by all means meant to make calculations easier but somehow that move made little sense when you were not cut for numbers. The other problem with Madam Zubeda was her lack of patience, so even with the help of sticks, would-be easy arithmetic seemed difficult. She would write an equation on the board and before anyone counted the first bunch, she would be shouting out people's names to give answers.

"Twelve times twenty . . . Lisimba!"

In such a case, that pressure forced the mind to shut down, and more often than not you would give the wrong answer. The result was instant thrashing. For reasons I have never understood, maths equations were always called problems. I started associating mathematics with problems and the cane. The subject freaked me out, made me feel stupid, and killed my confidence. A part of me died to mathematics, never to be resurrected even by the subsequent friendlier teachers.

All Hail Mr Mamesa!

Mr Jumba Mamesa was introduced to the school on assembly one cold morning, and something about him struck me. He was slender, not so tall, and donned a snow-white shirt, pitch-black pants and dark brown shoes with dangerously pointed fronts—sharp shooters. His hair was well-cut and trimmed. Even after the assembly his image lingered like a ghost that refused to be exorcised. It was like I had found a piece of me that was lost for eons.

We went to class for the day's lessons. I sat at my desk and waited for Madam Zubeda's imposing figure to storm in. Instead, the new teacher walked in. His pronunciation made English sound way cooler than anything I had learned since that first morning I learned doodling. He added intonation to his words, stressing what needed to be emphasized and relaxing on the negligible bits. He announced that he would be our English teacher, taking over from our now immediate former English teacher who was retiring. Language, check … style, check … youthfulness … check! English was reborn. Hillary was born. Life had new meaning!

Mr. Mamesa was likable, a favourite even when he punished us. He did not have to threaten us for vowels and tenses to stick. He did not ask us to kneel down on the cold floor or shout at those who failed to grasp some concepts. He, at no point, joined other teachers on the weekly disciplinary committees where pupils sat on one side, teachers the other then all mistakes committed would be read out and the culprits whipped in turns by each teacher. Mamesa was more student than teacher; he was part of us, and together we became as thick as thieves. He sparked inside us a new perspective of learning, a fresh passion for the language that had been muzzled for a while. I started living for English. As difficult as other teachers made life, English became the ointment that soothed all the irritations. On days Mr Mamesa was absent for whatever reason, I felt sickly, as though a part of me had been taken away.

He was not the conventional *Read with Us* or *Neighbours* teacher. We sung during English lessons, recited poems, had language competitions, debates—name it.

> *In and out, the bamboo forest*
> *In and out, the bamboo forest*
> *In and out, the bamboo forest*
> *Who will be my partner?*

We sang the song countless times, and every time it felt fresher than the first.

> *When I was walking, I met an elephant,*
> *The elephant told me, I want to dance with you!*

To the enjoyment of everyone in class, we enacted a scene in *Read With Us,* that involved a family pulling and pulling at a cassava until it came out and everyone fell with a thud.

One day, Mr Mamesa came to class and called out; "Nebert, picture this. One morning you wake up late, rush to the sitting room, gobble down a cup of tea then it burns your tongue. You go to the window and spit it all out. While this is happening, you are trying to fasten the buttons on your shirt, combing hair, and gathering books into your school bag. What do we call that kind of state?"

We tried a number of guesses, then he gave us the simplest answer I have ever heard for a question that cracked my head so much;

"You are in a great hurry, Nebert," that's the answer. No one ever forgot what a great hurry looked like since that day, even proven *dwanzis* (dumbs). Every class and school had one or more of those.

To English I was like a junkie, every lesson like a badly needed dose of methamphetamine. Mr Mamesa always brought us story books that we read and narrated the stories to the rest during lessons. We were a team working together as equals but captained by a wonderful young man in official wear. He taught us every subsequent year. Sadly, he was transferred to another school when I was in class 6, but the passionate love for English he had planted and nurtured inside me remained strong.

I don't even remember saying goodbye. We closed school one time, and when we came back from holidays, his position had been replaced. They should have consulted his students before transferring him, as he would have moulded us into the new generation Shakespeares. Years later, I heard that Mr Jumba Mamesa, my English champion, had not only passed on but was even buried. The news was broken sledgehammer way, leaving me to deal with the grief and mourn in my solitude.

Although Mr Mamesa was just doing what he enjoyed and was paid to do, I doubt he knew how much impact he had on me, us. He was touching a whole generation to come. In me he left a language orphan when he breathed his last.

Many years after the fact, I am still in denial and yet to heal from that loss. Etched in my heart are his footprints that will be carried to my own grave, never to be erased by the hands of time.

The only other subject that came close to the love I had for English was Kiswahili, taught by another jovial soul from the Coastal region where the language was born. His name was Ken Muhambi. His excellent command of Kiswahili laced with proverbs, sayings, and anecdotes from Mombasa, some too hyperbolic to be believable, always made moments with him worth looking forward to. Mr Muhambi was also a born artist, one of those talented cartoonists who are never discovered. Most of his lessons thrived on illustrations, like a movie storyboard, which made his lessons easy to understand. He was good looking by all standards—athletic body, light complexion, always dressed in smart casual. Whenever he went to visit his people at the Coast, he brought a coconut to class, which we would break and divide it amongst us.

Mr Muhambi made us write lots of *insha*. They would revolve around a quotation or a proverb that you needed to infer and write a story on, or a continuation of an already started story. This continuation was a bit tricky if you missed out on the hidden expectation from the onset, as you would blubber about things that didn't make sense and give yourself six out of thirty marks for getting your name, class, and school right.

Kiswahili rejected Benard Buluku, one of my classmates, and it never changed its mind.

The instructions were simple: write an *insha* with the title *Kikulacho Ki Nguoni Mwako*. This literally translated to 'the bug that bites you is in your own clothes'. There had to be a moral lesson at the end that you have to bring out write about friends who are close to you yet betray you.

Buluku wrote:

> *Kikulacho ni mdudu hatari.*
> *Akikuingia kwa nguo atakuuma usikie uchungu.*
> *Juzi kikulacho aliingilia rafiki yangu kwenye nguo. Nikamwambia, "Chunga kuna kikulacho nguoni mwako!"*
> *Hakuniskia.*
> *Ilipofika jioni alikuwa amevimba mwili wote.*
> *Funzo: Lazima tujihadhari sana na kikulacho.*

Mr Muhambi read it out aloud before the whole class as an example of what not to write. We laughed so hard, and from that day on, Buluku earned the nickname 'Kikulacho.'

Boy got four marks, out of thirty. What a Return on Investment!

Now, as fate would have it, Muhambi's good looks, amazing Kiswahili, and athletic body soon became the source of his woes. Turns out that the ladies (both students from our school and random villagers) crushed on him like tons of bricks. A list was released. I have always believed they were just crushes that took it a little too far, but then no one can tell where a man walks under the cover of darkness. Again, what can a boy, hardly fifteen years old, know about his teacher's after-school endeavours?

News of the never-ending fist fights in the area for him reached the district education office. He was transferred to I don't know where, and apparently died later on during my confused post-primary school years when I was stuck between boy and man.

School buses have revolutionized how children go to school. Nowadays, they are picked from different locations and delivered as a bunch to school, so if the bus arrives late it is the driver who is answerable. It was man for himself during our time. You arrived alone, therefore fully responsible for your lateness. Life was more difficult for children whose parents skipped schools nearer and enrolled them kilometres away. The intention may have been good, because performance is what mostly informed such decisions, but the burden of arriving in school on time was shouldered by the pupil.

Back then, we went to school in the morning, went back home for lunch, came back for the afternoon lessons then back in the evening. How children who lived far off they managed to concentrate in class the whole morning, run around the school compound at break time and still have energy left to go for lunch and back barefoot is a mystery. I always struggled to make it to school on time yet I lived not far away. I wondered what time those who lived far away had to wake up, prepare, have breakfast, and still make it in time.

Perhaps the one wrong thing the Ministry of Education allowed in that era was corporal punishment, even for mistakes like coming to school late regardless of how far you came from. Not that they did not know shoes were a luxury to over ninety-five of the students, nor that the village had no street lights therefore risky for children to walk to school that early. They made going to school a herculean task even for those who were passionate about education.

Mondays were the days with the highest number of latecomers. How your week was depended on the time you arrived in school on Monday. School prefects aided and abetted teachers in making your week miserable by standing at the strategic school entry points and noting down those who were late. On most occasions, ninety-nine percent of the student population made it to those list more than once. The lists were then forwarded to the teacher on duty just before we went in for the morning remedial class, who would choose to either give punishment immediately or read them out during assembly.

One of the most difficult weeks was when Mr Alumasa was on duty. Whoever walked through the school gate after him—even if it was 5 a.m.—was considered late and eligible for punishment. You would struggle so much to wake up early, skip breakfast and run all the way to school only to see a long queue of pupils lying heads down at the school entrance. You had the option of joining them awaiting punishment or changing course by hiding in one of the many bushes nearby, keeping track of proceedings as you planned on how to sneak to school unnoticed. Hiding in the bush was only beneficial if you did it without being discovered, so you hoped that no sneaky school neighbour would spot and frog march you to the staffroom … and there was no shortage of sneaky neighbours.

One day, I sprinted all the way from home only to spot Mr Alumasa gathering students at the gate. He had not spotted me, or so I hoped, but I decided I was not going to join the group. I had not woken up too early to get punished. Was 6am late? I dashed to the usual hiding bush behind the school, did my squat then plotted the next move. I could see more and more students running to Mr Alumasa, getting their five strokes of the cane and going to class. At one point, I considered surrendering and getting over and done with it, but I was not one to rescind on my decisions. In my head, forces of good and bad were at war: one reprimanded me for trying fate while the other stood by the idea that I would be foolish to put in all that effort then still surrender to the cane. My heart palpitated and pounded like a mill, I was worried it would jump out of my chest. My skin was all goose bumps, blood boiling such that even with the chilly temperatures, my palms dripped with sweat.

Do I just go man? I asked myself.

'No! Mr Alumasa is pushing things too far,' the devil whispered in my ear.

Well, the devil won. Nonetheless, an opportunity to sneak behind Mr Alumasa when he was distracted did not present itself as I had envisioned. I waited, nothing. 6.30a.m. … 7:00a.m … 7:30a.m … 8:00a.m! By the time the assembly bell sounded, I was still sitting behind the bush, the morning cold now biting, my palms clammy and every part of me going numb with regret. This was it; my day to drop out of school had finally come.

I did some quick calculations: *Go back home … and do what? No, bad idea.* Our village had snitches rutting out truants every other day. That none of them had spotted me in the bush for all those hours was enough luck for the day. I could not get lucky longer. *How about the river nearby? There are guava trees you can hide under and sit on, like a leopard, then walk back home over lunch hour like you just came from school. Brilliant idea!*

Things went well as far as I was concerned, to the point of locating the tree that could offer me the best concealment. I wished. Turned out someone had seen me and snitched me out to Mom, complete with my exact location.

I first thought I was dreaming when I heard my name being called by a commanding voice I had heard a thousand times. Under the tree stood Mom, her gaze fixed on me. Her look told it all; I was to either get down the tree and face her wrath or get down and face her wrath! I obliged, prepared psychologically for the long day ahead. It was only mid-morning but I felt like I had lived for a whole week between waking up and that moment. The kicks and slaps did not stop as she escorted me all the way to school. She was stopped countless times by whoever we met and asked what her young man had done. She would explain, share *a tete-a-tete* then continue slapping me. I wished for the earth to open up its jaws and swallow me alive, but well, *siku ya nyani ikifika kila mti huteleza.*

"*Wewe* (slap) *kazi yako* (kick) *ni kutoroka shule* (slap), *si ndio?* (slap slap) *Unajua* (slap) *vile tunasumbuka* (kick) *kulipa fees?* (slap) *Eeh?* Hillary! (slap)

I was presented on a silver platter to Mr Alumasa. He stood there smiling, thirsting for my blood. This was going to be a serious case, and punishment was direct death or something very close … which would still end up in death. I made a silent prayer, like the Biblical thief on the cross beside Jesus, that God would forgive and accept me into His Kingdom.

Mr Alumasa asked me to sit down, disappeared and re-appeared with the deputy head teacher! Now the situation was deteriorating fast: I was getting nailed on the cross by two people, TWO!

"Hillary," the Deputy started.

"Yes?"

"What is happening? Even you? A position one every term can skip school and go hide?"

Mom stood there, giving me that eye I hated. This was an unexpected turn of events by all means. A student being given a chance to respond to a case before being 'murdered' was a lifeline I wasn't sure how to clutch on, it didn't happen this side of the Sahara. When you were in the dock in the court of adults, you were guilty as charged.

I composed myself and went ahead to explain everything as exactly as I could remember that morning. It was like a little court session; the School versus Hillary, with the plaintiff being my own mother. Representing myself, I told the esteemed court that by all standards I did not come to school late, that 6 a.m. was still too early for any primary school kid to be categorized as late, and that it was unfair to put so much effort into keeping time and get beaten at the end of it. My emphasis was on the fact that deciding lateness based on the time the teacher on duty arrived was finding reason to punish students but nothing educational. I added that the school had instilled fear instead of respect in us, and turned teachers into bullies rather than our protectors. It is this fear that made us tolerate punitive legislation without voicing our concerns because we lacked a listening ear. At that point I did not care. What could have gone wrong had gone wrong anyway. I was already in the dock and punishment was guaranteed.

I was heard!

Would you believe it? I was not just let scot-free for standing up against an uncouth law, but an announcement was made on assembly that 7 a.m. was the official time to be in school. Anyone walking into school from 7.01a.m. onwards was late, earlier than that was good time. I may have put my life and future on the line, but my little way changed a draconian law, without a single placard, nor student demos. Every time I remember that morning, I blame myself for not nurturing the lawyer in me. I would probably have grown into one of the most revered lawyers this world has seen.

Blame it on Mr Mamesa, he made me see Literature as my
forever end game.

27

CHAPTER 3

MEET 'MARGARET THATCHER'

THE WORLD KNOWS Margaret Thatcher as not only Britain's first female Prime Minister, but also for her rigid and uncompromising political views. This stand earned her the title 'The Iron Lady'. Madam Jane Ambani, the woman who gave birth to me, was a total replica of that Thatcher character, at least in word and deed.

If early years' photos are anything to go by, she was a gorgeous petit damsel with a modelesque body in her maiden years. By the time I was born, the years had turned her into a slightly dark sizeable woman with a no-nonsense face. She retained the natural black African hair that was always combed into a flowing curl that fell on her upper back. Mom loved floral dresses, her favourite being blue and red flowers. A beautiful mushy woman from early on, I think I know why my old man saw her and put an end to his search for a lifetime partner. She is sarcastic, in a very annoying way. She must have picked it from her own mother, our *Guku,* who is one of the most wonderful women I have set my eyes on.

Mom was a P1 teacher then, a career she always told me she settled for because they grew up in so much squalor that when she finished high school she knew her education journey had come to an end. However, a Good Samaritan offered to pay her tuition, and the only option being teaching college. You should hear her highlighting how she plans to follow that dream of becoming something bigger, like the country's president, now that she has some money. That makes me scared, very scared. Having grown up by her side, I pray that her dream never comes true. Being woken up with whips just when the early morning dream was hitting high gear for a mistake you made the previous day or earlier and played hide and seek until bedtime hoping she would let go was tough. No, she didn't, not even if you avoided her for a whole week. The only way to get away with a mistake in that compound would have been to walk around dressed like an Eskimo, then sleep during the day when she was away at work. Otherwise, the five or so minutes you let your guard down, a slap fell on your face. Those slaps were so hard your eyes would be wide open but all you could see was total darkness as your head spun in circles.

Only teachers' kids can relate with how difficult it is to be in the same school your mom or dad teaches. It is like a little prison, an extension of your home. Every move you make is usually seen through the eyes of your parent; you become some sort of 'big brother' to everyone, because you are a teacher's child. It was an unforgivable crime to make a mistake in school because it tainted her name. After the high expectations placed on pastor's children, the next category is teacher's children.

Mom taught Art and Craft in my class. It always felt to me like there was tension between us during her lessons, probably because she always gave me those eyes of 'try anything stupid and see me kill you now'. Another tricky bit was that whenever we had exams and she released the results, fellow students always looked at my score at the corners of their eyes. It was like they suspected I was given a leakage or my paper marked with some leniency. They didn't know that she was too harsh to even let anyone near her home office. None can live some of these moments for long; suicide would be the way out.

Away from school, I have always seen myself as an ex-convict from the Madam Jane Correctional Facility, so much that even in adulthood, with all the beards, I am still paroled. The good thing about being in such a set-up is that you are forced to always think way ahead of the 'officer' and circumvent the system.

Being denied food as punishment was the norm in our household. However, it was illegal for you to decide not to eat. Being locked out of the house for you to meditate on your mistake was acceptable, but staying out on your own to do the same meditation was a crime. It was basically the way Kenya operates now; change the constitution to fit this particular project, someone capitalizes on the same loophole for a contrary gain then everyone is up in arms about how people need to adhere to the constitution. See that? My mom should have been a politician; I have never doubted her sentiments.

Mom, or let us stick to Thatcher, was not very receptive to ideas on the family meal plan from anyone else. She was like an African government procurement officer; sending out requests for prospective suppliers to apply for tenders but with an already existing decision.

"Unataka tukule nini leo?"

"Mimi nataka tukule nyama."

"Ooh. Sawa. Si babako ako na butchery *huko Mbale? Enda ulete kilo mbili kutoka huko."*

Of course Dad never even dreamt of operating a butchery, let alone owning a butcher's knife. In fact, I have never seen him move close to anything being slaughtered. I therefore concluded that he sees us, slitting animal throats, as murderers of some sort. He never gets late when meat is on the table though; hands already washed, probably even prayed 10 minutes before the meal arrives on the table.

Thatcher also loathed her child walking in an outfit that was either too loose or faded.

"Hillary! Tembea kabisa na nguo imetoboka kwa sababu wewe ni yatima!"

"Madam Jane alikufa akaacha watoto wakihangaika."

Earning her trust was another uphill trust. I knew this was a lost cause when I observed a trend on Sundays. She would give you a five-shilling coin for offering at the church, but throughout the service her eyes would be fixed on you, taking them off you when her participation in the church choir was required. These gazes were to deter you from walking out in case you were tempted to visit the shop opposite the church compound to buy sweets with the offering money. This was done against the backdrop of her repeated warning that if you ever 'ate' God's money, He would plant a huge pumpkin on your forehead as punishment. Either she knew her threat was far-fetched, or she believed that her son was willing to risk a pumpkin forehead in favour of sweets.

She pursued further education and moved from the P1 category to Special Education, which also meant that she had to change schools and give us 'breathing space' at school. It was also a perfect opportunity for Tope and I to break away from that 'Madam' bondage, build our individual identities and successfully live double lives. On the outside, we were the good, well-behaved 'Madam's protégés' but on the inside we were afflicted with misdemeanour, felony, mischief, and recklessness.

32

CHAPTER 4

WELCOME SHOES

MBALE IS MY hometown, the first town I opened my eyes to during my road to discovery. It was not so big then ... well, it still isn't. It is a dwarf town, if anything like that exists. You can walk from one end to the next in less than 30 minutes. It is basically a few rows of old buildings hopelessly begging for fresh coats of paints or demolition altogether. A few high-rise structures have crept in over the years as more and more of my people make it big in the job market.

Although it was a 20 minutes' walk from home, the town was out of bounds for most of us. It was even officially a crime at school to be found at Mbale unless it was Sunday and you could prove you were headed to or from church. It was tricky for those fellow schoolmates who lived near town because they could not avoid roaming those streets after school. They ended up being victims of lashing every other day for being spotted 'idling around Mbale in school uniform.'

Idamugu, Tope's classmate, was the greatest culprit. You would have thought the boy owned a stall in some part of the town. I bet he even got used to being spotted and beaten the following day. One of the things that made the rest of us go to Mbale was buying poorly cooked but addictive *vitumbua* and *simsim* sold for one shilling. The former were made of fermented maize flour, sold on an open basin and exposed to all the dust being blown around, but when they landed on your tongue, the taste was incomparable. They looked like fingers; same width, same 'complexion', same length. *Simsim* was a mix of boiled sesame seeds and fried groundnuts, wound into neat round balls that had an irresistible aroma you could sniff from meters away. Unhygienic as they were prepared and displayed on the market, I never heard of a case to do with a stomach upset, or diarrhoea. It is like our systems had embraced whatever garbage made its way into the mouth. What was good for the mouth was excellent for the stomach.

Saturday is market day in Mbale, the day most dwellers do their weekly shopping at the open-air market, and businesses make a kill. It is also a source of livelihoods for many people. I know at least five who have been raised, clothed and educated by proceeds from those dilapidated stalls in market. It boasts of heaps of dirt, and humongous rats the size of a puppy, some living in an underground hole right next to the stall of the guy who has been selling rat poison for years, and you thought impunity was only in the government?

The women who do business in the unchanging Mbale's open-air market are hardworking and they have been there for as long as I can remember. Most of the food sold at the market comes from farms around save for fish which is supplied from Kisumu, a short distance away. The textiles and shoes—new and used—are mostly 'imported' from Nairobi in bales … and that is where my dalliance with shoes begins.

Thatcher made me wake up earlier than usual on this particular Saturday morning, then took me on a walk to Mbale. For a woman who was the queen of promising a walk with you then sneaking out as you struggled to locate your shoes, this was suspicious. The moment I saw her patiently wait for me to dress up, I knew she was up to something, but played the innocent trusting son and followed like a sheep being led to the abattoir by the shepherd.

The walk to the market was uneventful, save for her usual stops and chit-chats with villagers. My job description at the market, though not explained to me, was to pick the shopping; fish here, onions there, tomatoes at the other stall, sugar from that shop and shove it into a plastic bag she had asked me to carry from home.

The next stop was at a Bata shop. I had not seen so many shoes in one place before; shoes with flowers, plain white shoes, shoes with huge soles, shoes with long noses, shoes with laces, some without. I was mesmerized. How possible was it that Mbale had all these shoes yet ninety percent of the people I knew walked barefoot? I was asked to push my foot into a transparent plastic bag then tried close to five different pairs arranged before me. There was this distinctive smell about the new shoes, one that has been stored somewhere in my long-term memory since that day. I kept poking my feet in and out of different pairs, until Thatcher found one that she thought looked good on me. After haggling with the attendant, one black pair with a high rubber sole and wide laces running through little holes on the top was stashed neatly in a red box and handed to me. She paid, and *voila!* . . . I had my first ever pair of school shoes.

I imagined myself going school come Monday with that pair completing my look. I pictured fellow pupils admiring me, including those that hated me for whatever reason. *I had arrived!* No other pupil in my class had shoes, I was going to be the boy every girl wanted to hang out with. For the first time, I felt that Thatcher had boosted my confidence—something she had never done. At that moment, I felt on top of the world, untouchable, but there was a problem … while I was bursting with excitement and the urge to get home and try out the newest member of my collection, Mom did not seem to be in a hurry.

When you have a tyrant mother, you learn to follow close behind, silent, like a dog. At some point, my excitement was replaced with regret, as my instincts picked up what seemed to be a not so good ending to this day.

Vihiga Rural Health Centre, simply known as the 'Centre,' was located directly opposite what was those days two famous business outfits in Mbale—Mungoma Chemist and Kodak Studio. Mungoma was famous because everyone went there for Panadol and Malaraquine, two drugs that treated every ailment that came our way. You had stomach ache, run for Panadol from Mungoma; headache, that's malaria, go grab some Malaraquine. The Kodak studio is where everyone in the village visited to have their photos taken for memorabilia after every event that was considered serious.

One January, after spending the holiday at grandma's, we took a photo at Kodak Studio and though I did not come out looking good (as usual), it has to this day reminded us of that evening. The cameraman 'arranged' us next to a huge pile of blue and red plastic flowers, ordered us to smile, counted down from five and clicked the shutter. Thanks to film technology then, there was no benefit of preview. After two weeks, the results were out; somehow my eyes had developed a mind of their own and shut the moment he clicked away. Everyone else in the photo had a bright smile while I stood there looking like a zombie. To spite me, Thatcher went ahead and mounted that photo on a glass frame and propped it on the wall right in the middle of the sitting room so that every visitor was made aware of my worst of my awkward moments. It is the reason I chose to be in the media but behind the scenes—my enmity with the lens goes back into time.

The good and obedience son I was, I walked beside Thatcher, thinking that we were headed to the studio for a chance to redeem my image and take a replacement photo, but we passed it. Our walk took a left turn, heading to the one place we all hated—the Centre! Soon as we walked past the row of women selling bottles to patients with which they would carry syrup with, the smell of medicine, antiseptic and methylated spirit stung my nose. Straight ahead was a long row of wooden benches with people; some seated, others looking lost, and a majority lying there with hopeless faces.

The local title for nurses was 'Sister,' I am told because once upon a long time ago clinical facilities were run by churches which propagated the use of the line 'Sister-in-Christ'. They wore sky-blue dresses with a white hem around the neck and a nurse's white cap sticking out of their black African hair at the centre of the head. They moved up and about; some with files, others pushing stretchers, others patrolling the corridors with a devilish twitch of their not-so-plump bottoms. For some reason, ladies that era did not have hips and behinds like they do nowadays, it was a generation where people appreciated what was offered as it came.

We sat at an empty bench. Clearly, I had been brought to hospital for a sickness I was not aware of. Then again I was with Thatcher, so she was probably the one coming for treatment and here I was getting worked up for no reason.

From where we sat, a closed blue door written 'RECEPTION' stood unmoved right ahead, an open louvered window adjacent to it. With benefit of hindsight, it is through the louvers that patients explained how their bodies were behaving as notes were taken down by a Sister. The notebook was passed over to another Sister who would go through the information then usher in the patient for either further diagnosis or treatment.

Sitting on that waiting bay was in itself medication. You watched people in worse conditions come in and you got better. Sitting there for ten minutes was enough to watch as accident victims, survivors of house fires and some who were bleeding from random village fights streamed in, and since there was no ambulance, most patients were brought aboard bicycles, wheelbarrows, or jalopies that operated as taxis. I still remember word going round that one of the kids who had been stretchered in screaming her lungs out had somehow got hold of her mother's giant scissors and chopped off one of her fingers. The medics were at that point struggling to find ways of attaching the severed part.

Even though you sat next to people puking and writhing in pain, it was difficult to hear of modern-day giants like HIV/Aids, Cancer, or gunshot cases. We trusted each other so much that needles and syringes were used, boiled in hot water to kill germs and re-used.

I could not shake off the feeling that we were not here for Mom but me. History had shown that 99.9% of the times we walked through the Centre gates, I walked out with nursing needle pains on my buttocks. I was right, and this was probably worse than I had imagined. Instead of being called into the usual injection room, a 'sister' came and asked us to follow her to a side I had never had a chance to explore.

This visit may have been shrouded in mystery to this minute, but it was as clear as day that things were spiralling out of control while I watched and I could do nothing about it. That they were taking me to the farthest and most hidden room of the hospital was a bad sign ... but I was not sick! What was wrong with these two women?

Every step we made led us closer to wherever it was we were going, making my head spin. I was struggling to hold back tears, trying to hold myself together lest the tyrant's kicks and blows landed on me. The easiest option would have been to bolt out of that facility as though I had seen a demon and disappear through the rat-infested corridors of Mbale, but then I would have to end up back home, with the same woman I had escaped from. So, I stayed on.

When we finally got into the room, I knew this was surgery. There were scissors all over the table right from the entrance; some straight, some with slender blades, others with twisted ends. *Many* scissors. This was it. Mom must have decided I was becoming too naughty so my brain needed to be checked and any foreign materials removed. At that point, a eureka moment happened. THE SHOES! Those shoes, that black pair that had made my morning, was actually a bribe to lure me into this and not an actual gift. I had exchanged my happiness for a pair of shoes! My stomach muscles went taught, my heart started to flutter. Everything in me burnt. On this one, the tyrant had won. She had played me, and like a moth trooping towards the light I got right into the trap. That is how fish get baited and caught— foolishness, or greed, *or both*. I, from that minute, hated that pair of shoes. That had been my bait, the reason I was now in an abattoir like a pig. This was what mothers who were fed-up with misbehaving kids did to silence them.

The 'sister' gave me a transparent plastic toy to play with, a second bribe in a span of an hour. The toy felt like the kiss Judas planted on Jesus before handing him over to the people who would crucify him. I hated it too. A jovial man in a white coat approached us. At least another man was in the mix, I felt slightly safe. A man would understand me better. He asked about school, my friends, then requested to look into my mouth with a small black torch. Torches are harmless, I thought, not unless this one happened to go up in flames and burnt my mouth, so I opened, wide. Why a grown man was scavenging through a young boy's mouth was a question I struggled to answer, but wouldn't wait for long.

The man switched off the torch, put on surgical gloves on his hands and, guess what …? He took a pair of the long scissors and sat right across me! I was praying he doesn't tell me to open my mouth again, because the brain surgery I had thought about was better, this one looked like my tongue was on the line, because what else could be cut using scissors in the mouth?

He did exactly that; asked me to open my mouth then went ahead to shove the scissors and some ugly spoon inside while the 'sister' held up the torch! I prayed to God that if he was chopping off my tongue he leave a bit for me to still eat *mandazi,* then closed my eyes and waited for the worst. He actually chopped something, because I felt a sharp pain in my throat. He then pulled out both the scissors and spoon. I was dead. I knew I was.

I was shown a sink on the wall and told to go spit all the blood there. I was then given some liquid to gurgle and spit, then told to wash my mouth with lots of water. My tongue felt intact; what had these guys just chopped off from my throat?

"*Hiyo tumekata inaitwa kilimi,*" the 'sister' explained.

Whatever that was.

"Mom, what was that?" I asked when we got home.

"You had *tondos.*"

"What is *tondos?*"

"It is some growth that occurs in your epiglottis. They make someone thin, and if not chopped off, the growth could soon block the whole throat.

"And what causes *tondos?*"

"Tondos are caused by too much sugar."

"Too much sugar from where?"

"It means you've been stealing my sugar and licking it, so it's God's way of punishing you."

I let that story die, but I was still furious at how the whole issue had been handled. I did not have to be bribed to go to receive God's punishment, and Sunday school had taught me that punishment will be meted on us in hell, not by some smiling guy in a white coat and scissors. They had never told me in Sunday school that God's punishment was this harsh, so if I continued stealing sugar the next punishment could even be death. I wasn't giving God another chance to punish me. I made a promise to myself that however sweet those crystals looked, I was not going to poke my fingers into the sugar dish again. It has taken me years to understand that *tondos* was Luhyia for tonsils.

Monday came, and though I still loathed the shoes, they opened curtains to a new era in walking to school. An era of shoes. An era of moving on a bribe every day of the week. I, for the first time since that Black Saturday, took time to carefully look at the shoes, like a Crime Scene Investigator scrutinizing what is expected to be crucial evidence. It was evidence of a bribe anyway. There was a sticker inside written Bata Bullets. I had been so annoyed to realize they had a name, and not a bad one. They were a perfect fit when I tried them on, and they made me feel a few inches taller. Some oomph had been pumped into my life, and though I did not like the sound of it, truth was the shoes looked great on my feet. Give the devil its due; I hated them but they were a beautiful bribe.

Turns out I was not the only one that had issues with the pair; *everyone else* at school did. The looks I got the moment I walked into the school compound spoke volumes: I had broken tradition, mutilated acceptable school dress code.

First, the sanitation prefect slapped me for not washing the allocated washroom to the standard he expected. He blamed it on the shoes, said that I was doing it hurriedly so that I do not soil them. Then another pupil complained during assembly that I had stepped on his big toe and disturbed the usually quiet jigger inside. After that, I was picked to go lead the morning prayers because I was looked more of a teacher than a pupil.

Class was no different: the first lesson maths and Madam Zubeda asked the day's first question, looked around the class for someone to assign and shouted "Yes, the boy with shoes!"

The question jolted me from space back to earth; I had no idea what the question was let alone the answer. Interestingly, the annoying pair of shoes made everyone forget my name. Madam Zubeda set precedence, and every teacher who came after her called out to me to answer questions or give an opinion.

After what seemed like eternity, the last bell of the day rang. The relief was debilitating. I walked home with voices in my head saying 'young man, boy, shoes, you, yes you, shoes this, shoes that.' The voices were so cacophonic that I had a bad headache, not forgetting the canes I had received from five teachers. A sharp pain tore through my scalp, from the forehead to the nape, and it was Monday.

That day I was the only pupil in class. I had answered all the questions, given opinion on topics I was hearing about for the first time, been scorned and laughed at enough to last me a lifetime. To think they were shoes I had hated from the onset, and that I was still expected to go to school the following day in them was enough to make me want to run away from home! I made a decision that evening; I was dropping the idea of shoes from that day. I would wear them over the weekend or when I was going somewhere that really needed shoes, but in school? Nah.

Mom sometimes behaved like a ghost. She would appear at the most unexpected time in the most unexpected fashion! It happened the next morning. Ordinarily, she never came out to inspect or check on how I dressed or went to school, she just knew I would. That morning, in what remains one of my life's biggest question marks, Mom did. I was just dashing out of the house for the sprint to school when her shout stopped me right in my tracks.

"Irisimba!"

"Ehe"

"Kuja hapa!"

I dragged myself back to where she was a standing, arms akimbo.

"Viatu ziko wapi?"

"Kwa nyumba."

"Ooh. Nyumba siku hizi iko na miguu inavaa viatu."

"Tembea kwa umande kabisa ukuwe mgonjwa nishikwe na stress *nikufe ndio ufurahi. Tembea!"*

I said nothing.

"Umeamua hii nyumba sitawahi ishi kwa amani."

She continued to rant.

"Vaa hizo viatu vile unataka! Babako si amepanda mti wa pesa kwa hii compound *huwa nachuna nikununulie vitu?"*

I walked back into the house, head down, and the cursed pair of shoes. I lost count of the humiliation, scorn, hate and bullying I put up with because I had shoes while the rest did not. It was killing me inside as days moved on.

"You have shoes and you don't even know the answer!"

"You, the one with shoes, stop looking behind and answer!"

"Stop dragging your shoes on the floor!"

"The boy with shoes, what's your opinion?"

"Young man, please step out of class and wipe your shoes on the grass. They are leaving dirt marks on the floor."

Those and many more were quips I endured every day. For years, my namesake, Hillary Membe, and I were differentiated by 'the madam factor' so people would always qualify mine as "Hillary wa Madam Jane" while Membe was just Hillary. I was now officially 'the boy with shoes' in the school, people only remembered my real name when the exam results were read out.

What a pair of shoes could do to a primary school kid in Africa in the late 20th Century! At some point, my endurance ran out and I was forced to come up with a plan B, and it worked well. I would wear them at home, remove and put them in my bag just before getting to school then slide them back on on the way home. Thatcher was happy, fellow students were happy, teachers remembered I was Hillary and not the boy with shoes, win-win.

I had shoes, but I did not have shoes.

CHAPTER 5

NEW FRONTIERS

THE YEAR 1993 almost took me off course. I made new friends, wrote my first good composition, and … discovered money! When you mentioned money in our class, one name stood out like a sore thumb—Alfred. He was that guy, the Big Cahuna. He, on many occasions, used this 'wealth' to get his way. He paid Nebert, the class mathematics geek, to do his assignments daily; paid Hussein, the class prefect, not to include him on the list of noisemakers; and paid the rest of us to be his friends. Whatever was left from his deep coffers was given out as soft loans to those in need. Problem was, Alfred took promises seriously. If you promised to pay on a particular day, he would remind you a day earlier that he expected his money back the following morning. If you brought it, you were safe, and increased your loan limit. He was a little human bank.

Those who defaulted Alfred's loans were in some of the worst positions anyone that age could be. He would begin by alienating you from the rest of the world, gather a group of boys to waylay you on your way home and descend on you with kicks and blows. Victims of Alfred's goons would not report the incident for fear of: one, being punished for '*kuombaomba pesa kama chokora*'; two, after rutting on him, he would get punished then come back more annoyed at you. Why would you want to dig your own grave? No one wanted that; so, you would kill that vibe and walk home as though nothing had happened. The worst was joining his list of 'send offs' which was school closing day beating to send you home for the holiday with bruises and swellings. It was the culmination of letting out all the anger that had been piled up during the school term to pave way for a new term with new mistakes and new anger.

As careful as I had been all along, as good a boy as I had tried to be in school, I found myself owing Alfred. It was dumb that I had gotten into debt at that early age, it was dumber that the repayment date had come so quick without me noticing, but it was dumbest that on the eve of the due date when the reminder was made, I had absolutely no idea where I was going to get the money.

Thatcher was in the kitchen when I got home that evening. I tried to think of a good story to extract money from her but nothing came up. In any case, she needed so much convincing to give you money and even then, it would be monitored like a patient on life support. The lie many told their parents when they wanted money was that it was for some school trip, but history had showed that Mom took such cash to the class teacher *herself*. Option two was borrowing, but I would subject myself to thorough scrutiny and questions on why I wanted the money. The worst option sufficed—stealing. It seemed easier; no questions and (hopefully) no drama. Every time I was at crossroads, the devil always kicked into action way before heavens could present a second alternative.

I snuck to her bedroom. Her handbag hung on the headrest of the seat beside the bed. My hands trembled precariously they couldn't hold anything, and sweat drenched my whole body. I had never stolen from my parents, but the image of Alfred and his goons killing me overrode ethics. The circumstances at hand were too huge to handle, I had my body to protect and the only way out was by having the money.

I slid my hand into the first pocket, nothing. I heard footsteps from a distance. I stopped to listen. They faded out. False alarm, but that was a wake-up call that I needed to get it done away with before actual footsteps came. I quickly frisked through the bag and felt some coins at the bottom. Eureka! I fumbled with my fingers to follow them as they kept rolling away and finally held onto them. I fished out what my fingers were holding—three shillings. I considered going back for more but decided against it. I would take the three bob to Alfred for a start then promise to clear the balance of six shillings after a short while. Son of man was learning early how to manoeuvre bank loans in years to come.

Subsequent stealing episodes became easier, translating to a habit. A few days later, I stole again to clear Alfred's debt. It became addictive, and I let my guard down so much that I was soon discovered. That is the problem with being a *klepto*. You, after a while, start feeling invincible and do your thing with impunity. I happened to steal on a day I was the only one at home and so all evidence pointed at me. I had never thought of developing a solid alibi before committing the heist. I got a thorough clobbering for it, but not enough to cure me of my thieving habit. I was too deep in it. I would steal, get caught, receive my beating then plan to be more careful next time to avoid being caught.

The sad bit about my being a seasoned and addicted thief is that I stole to buy useless things like *mandazi*, sweets, and other confectionaries. Some guy called Dan had conveniently opened a café right outside the school compound, and the aroma that invaded our classes in the morning as he fried the *mandazi* drove me crazy. But, parents didn't pack snacks for us then nor give us pocket money, you left home as you were, and went back the same way. Even the dead are buried with some clothes despite being born naked! So, stealing bridged that gap, now that the only student in the whole school who already knew about side hustles was Alfred. The rest of us had the option of borrowing, lying, or my style.

Then came the day that I faced the worst of it all. Strangely, that was the one time I was not the culprit! I had been so engrossed in whatever was on my mind that I couldn't even remember the last time I had stolen from her. She discovered that her money was missing and the whole household knew who the suspect was. It is not a good thing to be a sure suspect for everyone in a family, because no one gives you the benefit of doubt. No one, even bothers, to listen to your cries for exoneration, and the few who give you an ear do it for the sake of listening, but they judge and crucify you in their minds even before you begin talking.

Mom called me to the main house and asked about her cash. I told her I had not seen it. She insisted that I was the only one in the household who stole her money, so it was obvious I had it. I was innocent, so I stood my ground and told her that I had not stolen it. She told me not to eat in that house until I produced her money from where I was hiding it. If I had some of my own money, I would have given her and moved on with my life, but I did not and since I had not stolen in a while, I was back to flat broke. My pleas of innocence were branded crocodile tears. Her mind was made up—I was to give her the money or know what she was made of.

"Nikigeuka hivi nipate pesa yangu hapa kwa meza!"

"Sijaiba pesa yako."

"Heeeee! Kwa hivyo mimi ni mjinga namba moja. Sijui pesa niko nayo?"

I was beaten that night with slippers, a belt, a piece of wood, a soda bottle, even a melamine plate! Mama Sharon, our now late neighbour, heard my wailing and came over to intervene. That knock on the door remains the most welcome and timely in my entire childhood; I probably would be crippled or dead by now. My whole body was swollen, parts of me were numb, and there were pockets of blood dripping from my gums. I could not even sleep that night; my body was on fire, and I had to wake up early for school the following day. I was heartbroken, crushed, angry, and bitter.

My Sunday school lessons came through in a big way that night. I asked God to help me get over the hate and bitterness I had in my heart, I could not even imagine how I would face and talk to Mom the next day knowing she almost killed me over money I knew nothing about. It was like everyone saw me as an outcast, the black sheep of the family. I even wished Mom had made good her earlier threat and abandoned me far away from home, I would have adapted to being a street boy. These thoughts, coupled with the pain all over my body, made me cry even more bitterly. At some point, I ran out of tears and just wheezed in pain inside the blanket.

The mystery behind the missing cash cleared some days later when someone confided in me that the money had been found. Turns out Thatcher changed bags and forgot to transfer the money. She did not apologize, perhaps out of guilt or just being Thatcher, most probably the latter. She has never known that I got hold of that secret, but as I grew up, I learned to let go of the past and forgave her. The bright side was that she had flogged the thieving habit out of me. I have to this day learnt to respect people's valuables.

CHAPTER 6

CRUSHING ON ESTHER

I HAD MY first crush during the Christmas holidays at my grandma's place. Her name was Esther. My aunt, Evelyne, was getting married, so all the young ones from the immediate family were pooled together and allocated positions to fill on the bridal line-up for the wedding day. Esther was not exactly a blood relative; she came from one of those households with very close family friends that either side is considered family. She landed a role because, as it turns out, my people give birth to more boys, so it was either girls from elsewhere be infused to fill the deficit or boys are matched up in pairs. The latter sounded creepy, especially in the 90s. I mean, how would my generation have taken the sight of two young men walking side by side in the wedding retinue on the aisle smiling sheepishly as they flash flowers around?

Esther was the right shade of chocolate, her skin as flawless and glowing as though God created her in the morning when He was fresh. For a girl growing up in the village where coconut oil, Bint el-Sudan, YU, and Solea were the only available hair and skin products, her baby-smooth skin and flowing hair were a sight to behold. The gap in her upper teeth lit up her whole face, accentuating the broad smile. She smiled at me during the introductions and I, for a moment, sat on that coveted seat right next to God. I guess Jesus had stepped out for a leek or something, but I swear I was there, beside the Maker, an angel flapping her wings while the Celestial Choirs crooned.

When she spoke, her voice knocked the remaining air out of me, sending me back to earth from the gates of Heaven. I was a whirlwind of everything: emotions, lust, and love—chaos. I could have sang *'some people wait a lifetime, for a moment like this,* but I did not know that song then. I am not sure I smiled back or just stared except that she was the most beautiful girl I had set my eyes on.

Esther was a goddess, the girl who became the ghost to haunt me and a reference point for the type of women that would interest me in my later years.

So, that holiday was all about the adults preparing for the big day and rehearsals. As though God was proving He really answered prayers, Esther was paired with me! From that moment, life had meaning. I knew I had found the woman of my dreams, the woman I was to marry when the time came. The people planning Evelyn's wedding would in not so long be back to do the same for Esther and Hillary.

So this is how Edward felt when he met Aunt Evelyn and proposed this wedding we were preparing for? I thought to myself, stealing lustful glances at my vixen whenever a chance presented itself. It is also the day I told myself that I would wed when time came. If this is what it meant for two to come together and be one, I was game. I even envisioned us in a kitchen, Esther cooking while I stood next to her holding a baby!

From that day, we rehearsed every evening outside grandma's house, followed by a meal then storytelling by my late aunt, Florence. I looked forward to going through the paces with Esther's soft palm locked in mine. I went to great lengths to please this daughter of Eve, honing vital skills for the future. I would pull seats for her, get her drinking water after the long round of rehearsals, say nice things to her and sit beside her throughout the meal and storytelling. Nonetheless, I was not allowed to sleep next to her, a brutal reminder that I was being stupid. Even before Aunt Florence finished telling us the day's stories, the girls would be whisked away to a different house to sleep, ensuring that at no point I had the chance to say goodnight to Esther.

Wedding line-ups were interesting: two boys held saucers with lit candles at the front, followed by two girls tossing flower petals around, then a boy and girl carrying the wedding rings. A matron carrying a lighter flanked the line-up, always looking out to re-light the candles that were on many occasions blown off by the wind. The wedding days, however, were not full of grandeur and as pompous as today. There was no hiring of tinted stretch limousines to impress the masses or intimidate others with. The cutting of the cake was done immediately after exchange of vows, no fabulous photoshoot moments nor transfer of guests to a different venue for the reception.

The food was hardly enough, and more than half of those in attendance, especially those in the middle, would miss the cake. Wondering how those in the middle missed cake instead of those at the farthest end? This is how— different bridesmaids would be dispatched to share the pieces of cake, some from the front and the rest from the back. They were to dish it out then meet at the centre so that everyone was served. Problem was that my people did not eat cake a lot, so the directive to strictly pick one piece was ignored as the plate moved around. Before you knew it, the maids were meeting at the centre both with empty plates. Even with such misgivings, weddings were still loved and well-attended because the essence was for the society to gather, officially hand over a smiling bride to a lucky gentleman and pray for a happily-ever after.

There were notable similarities with the modern day weddings, among them the existence of that one gloomy and bitter lady in the crowd, or two, depending on how many false marriage promises the groom had given during his dating days. There were cases of malicious exes pinching or tripping the bride as she made the walk down the aisle. Things were worse when the day's gloomy lady was a bridesmaid. She would try to hog the limelight by pushing to dress up better than the bride, forcing a smile when the camera pointed her direction but evidently annoyed at the bride's milestone. A good wedding cameraperson would notice and steal the real facial expressions when she wasn't aware capturing all eye-rolling episodes and freezing them forever.

If I thought Esther was beautiful, I had not seen her best yet; not until the wedding day. Her silk dress held onto her body, punctuating all her curves and edges. Her hair was blow-dried to a shiny sheen and combed straight back giving her a modelesque appearance; a feat accomplished with a metallic comb heated red on hot charcoal. Her face was a product of an expert makeup artist, the eyebrows trimmed and some shiny dots—whatever their name is—stuck on the right places. What was this if not heavens giving me a sneak peek into how *our* wedding would be? We even sat in the same car on the way to church!

While Esther was exuberant and excited about the day, I savoured the moment to keep brushing my neck against her hair. The feeling was like electric current running through me from head to toe, but I did not mind being electrocuted. My dreams were bursting at the seams at this particular moment, so much that to this day, I do not remember a single anything else apart from what I felt for Esther that day. When I think about it, I wonder how no one noticed that my neck had a huge oil smudge that morning yet I was clean shaven myself.

But the devil spoilt everything in his usual fashion: all the girls sat on a different row from us. Throughout the session, I only remember one boy who recited a poem to the couple, either because the poem was too stupid or that I thought I would 'borrow' him for the 'Esther Weds Hillary' day. Curtains came down on the wedding, and everybody watched as Evelyn wept while being hustled away in the 'Just Married' car. It was not a sleek limousine with tinted windows draped in enormous flowers and ribbons but the groom's dad's hatchback. It had not hit her that she would be headed to a new home immediately the final prayers were said, so she did not even get the chance to say her goodbyes to the people she was being separated from. One minute she was hanging around us, the next we could only see her hand wave through the rear window of the light-blue hatchback.

My eyes were heavy, the moisture in them coalesced to tiny droplets that made me take my eyes off Esther for a few seconds and when I regained my composure, she was nowhere to be seen. Just like Evelyn, I had lost my chance to have a final look at my Esther before we went separate ways. The difference between Evelyn and I was that whereas she had been separated from her people, she was headed for a new life with her husband. Hopefully, a better one and to make new experiences. I, on the other hand, was brutally separated from my crush, and there was no hope of a new life ahead. We were hurdled into some old school bus with a fussy driver threatening to leave people behind; the luxury of the saloon cars we had come to the church with were gone with the newlyweds and their entourage. Women dressed in beautiful assorted colours and big head gears sang joyfully and gyrated their hips to celebrate successful wedding. One of them would come up with a line mostly to tease the groom, shout it out then the rest would join in and turn it into a chorus.

Woman: *Edwardi yanyora hai isuti?* (Where did Edward get his suit?)

The rest: *Edwardi yasava baba isuti. Aziri muharusi. Eeeh eeeh eeeh eeeeh.* (Edward borrowed a suit from his dad. To wear on his wedding. Eeeh)

Woman: Aaah.

While everyone else was engrossed in the song, dance and ululation, I broke into a thousand pieces and no one seemed to notice. I needed something to assure me that I would see Esther again, even for a day. I realized that I had made two mistakes from the onset—not opening up and sharing my feelings when I had the chance and not finding out where she lived. I just knew her as a family friend on my grandma's side but had never taken visited her home, and asking about her home at such a time would have raised unnecessary eyebrows. I had seen enough arms akimbo from Thatcher, I did not want more.

The bus did not get us back to grandma's house. It had rained and the road impassable thus we made the torturous walk back home. During the long walk home without the cacophony of women teasing an absent newlywed couple I hatched a Plan B. It reminded me that Mr Mamesa had not taught me all that language to just stash in books and gather marks in exams. What is education if it cannot help you manoeuvre through such sticky situations? Brilliant! I was going to write Esther a letter and say all the things I had not said; my handwriting was neat and I was good at prose.

A few days after the wedding, we went back home—to Thatcher. That night, I sat at my bedside table, pulled out a blank page from my English exercise book and set it before me. My heart raced as I began to write:

Hi Esther,

I enjoyed the time we spent together during preparations for the wedding. I wish I could spend more time with you. I miss you so much, and would want you to be my girlfriend. I really like you a lot. Please reply.

Yours in love,

Hillary.

I may not have written much, but I envisioned how excited she would be at that letter. I could see the smile on her beautiful face as she read the words from my heart. But how was the letter going to get into the hands of the girl whose home I did not even know? Everyone else who had participated in the wedding and who would know her had to be a family member thus I couldn't use any of them as the postmaster. First of all, whoever I used to deliver my message had to be someone in my age bracket, and these people could not be trusted. These proxies had a tendency to use that secret to frustrate and arm-twist you into deals you probably would not agree to if you had no scandal under the table. Secondly, some good ones would keep the business dealing away from the public until the day you disagreed over an unrelated issue, then they would pour out all those details in the heat of the moment.

I was stuck, like a convict at the state penitentiary who plans and executes the perfect escape, only to successfully jump over the fence and realize they have no map of the area, no trusted contacts, no money, no civilian clothes, and no solid plan on how to stay on the outside without being re-arrested. How that delivery bit had eluded my mind I do not know. I had no way to deliver my letter to Esther. I was, however, confident that along the way I would conjure some magic and have it delivered. In the meantime, I would enjoy looking at it every time I opened my book and be reminded of an urgent but unfinished mission. I re-wrote it two or three more times to keep it fresh and added new words I picked during my English lessons.

One fine weekend, while I was away on an errand, Thatcher took our bags out for washing in preparation for the new week ahead. She had this habit of snooping through everything we had to kill a certain curiosity that we never understood. The moment I walked back home and saw my bag hung on the cloth line my heart sunk. I clutched on the slim glimmer of hope that she had this once emptied the bag and washed it without going through my books. The first person I met was Anne, my younger sister; one look at her and I knew my letter was in the wrong hands.

I did not even get time to deliver the report I had brought before I heard the dreaded call.

"*Hillary! Kuja hapa!*"

"*Nilikutuma* wedding *uende kutafuta wasichana?*"

Silence.

"*Umekuwa bubu, eeh?*"

More silence.

But what did she expect me to say, that "yes Mom I saw a beautiful girl and fell in love so you should start getting accustomed to a daughter-in-law with long flowing hair and the voice of an angel?"

Anything I would have said was against me in the court of Thatcher; so I kept mum. The angel of light on my right should have advised me to walk away quietly then approach her after she had cooled down to apologize, but the evil angel on my left told me not to dare to apologise. *If you dare go apologize you will just be stupid, there will be too many questions you cannot answer and the result will be another senseless beating anyway. Play hide and seek with her, don't get near her.*

True. You actually make sense. I hadn't thought about that. How can I be so stupid? I whispered back.

Saturday evening came and Mom and I had not been in close proximity. The plan was working wonders. I could see the devil winking at me for the job well done. On this one, we were winning.

Sunday, church, evening. The weekend was over! *Perfecto!*

Monday. *Wake up early, prepare, dash to school.* What a genius I had been. Then assembly time came, and that beautifully crafted house of cards came crashing down on me in shambles.

"*Kama unajua nywele yako ni refu, kumaanisha hukunyoa, baki ulipo,*" the teacher on duty said.

Jeez, I had forgotten that part of the weekend tradition was trimming hair, something Thatcher did on us with scissors she had owned since forever. She would make us kneel on the grass while she sat on a low chair, head on her lap, then she clipped your 'long' hair, running the scissors from one end of the head to the other, like a tractor harrowing land in preparation for the planting season. She would leave 'corn lines' on your head, but that was conventionally accepted as kempt hair in our school. Over the weekend, I had successfully avoided 'Esther questions' but skipped a vital tradition.

My punishment was splitting firewood, with a blunt axe, to be used by Mama Safi in the kitchen. This was meant to be a tedious exercise but on many occasions turned out exciting because you had time out of class, and in a group of other 'like-minded' lawbreakers cracking jokes and making fun of the whole situation as everyone played their role in clearing the load at hand.

"Hillary, mamako anakuja na atakupata ukifanya punishment."

I turned my head to see Thatcher in the distance headed towards the school staffroom. She looked unhappy, but hey, it had been two days since she pulled a *wikileaks* on me. My heart started to rise inside my ribcage, but because I had not been called to the staffroom nor told why she was there, I waited hoping against hope that all was good.

"Lisimba Hillary! Staffroom!" The deputy's call came.

The teachers were all seated in their respective seats, still preparing for their morning lessons. Most had cups of tea and maize cobs on plates placed before them. All eyes were fixed on me as I dragged myself in. The letter, in my neat handwriting—my carefully thought out words and signature—was at the middle of the table. One of the female teachers picked and read it out loud to the rest, causing a roaring laughter.

"And I see Ma-table has taught you well." Ma-table was bad slang for Mamesa, because *'mesa'* is Maragoli for 'table.'

Mr Mamesa sat at the farthest end, quietly watching the unfolding spectacle. He did not utter a word during the hullabaloo. I guess he was confused on whether to be proud that I was learning well or annoyed that I was using the same language to solicit for damsels.

"Na ujue kijana yako ako punishment," the deputy said.

"Punishment ya nini tena?"

"Huoni vile nywele yake inakaa ya mwenda wazimu?"

"Irisimba. Nimekosa makasi kwangu, sindio?" my mother asked.

My stomach muscles tightened.

"Mchape kabisa! Nimewapea ruhusa. Chapa hadi ashike adabu!" she continued.

Thatcher, in all her wisdom, threw me into the furnace like Shadrack, Meshack, and Abednego in the Bible. Even teachers who had no idea how the two cases I was in the dock for interlinked took the cane and took their turn at my bottom. As if that was not enough, I was made to read my letter publicly during assembly that evening as the whole school listened. I immediately earned the nickname 'Esther'.

I was told that news about my letter reached Esther's parents, and 'my love' was kind enough to deny any knowledge of such an arrangement. The Esther season ended on that low note. I still hope to see her again.

CHAPTER 7

BOYS AND TOYS

WITH MY ATTENTION off stealing cash and my Esther brutally stolen from me, my mind was idle. I had to find something else to get busy on, and as luck would have it, I developed an interest in vehicles. It began the day a truck delivered Nyayo milk to our school on a Friday afternoon. As the milk was being offloaded, I got busy reading everything written on the truck. Isuzu. TX. Ahaa, this truck was an Isuzu. That TX bit is what I did not understand. I approached the driver, leaning on the 'nose' and confirmed if Isuzu was indeed the name and added that he was surprised I gained interest in the truck whereas every other student was fixated on the milk in brown triangle packs. I almost told him I was nursing a bad heartbreak so milk did not make sense to me but decided against it. He let me get into the cabin, showed me a few things with names that sounded Irish then explained how each one worked in conjunction with another to move the truck forward, backwards, and sideways. I sat there like an apprentice taking in all the data on the dashboard, asking questions, and nodding when the answers were given.

From that day, I started reading all abbreviations and stickers pasted at the front and rear of vehicles and internalizing some names. I, for instance, noticed that there was a different truck from the one that delivered milk written Fuso, with another abbreviation as well. Then there was Nissan Diesel, with UD as the abbreviation. The weirdest I came across during that discovery period was a huge earthmover working on the road that led from Mbale into the village. It was yellow and mean with a huge bowl hanging under. The wheels wobbled from side to side, supporting an open-air driver's cabin perched on top of what looked like a huge arm. It was written Caterpillar. That was the most perfect name for a yellow monster with the flexibility and looks it boasted. I was mesmerized at the moves that machine was able to do without breaking a sweat … and the roar! When Thatcher, as though touched by the hands of an anger, granted me permission from home some weekends I would spend the day following the Caterpillar as it fell fences, sunk trenches and flattened rocks, leaving in its wake a new road.

The family cars came in three models: Datsun, Mazda, and the most common, Peugeot. I would have been hard-pressed to know the name was French and should be pronounced as "POOzho", so I settled to what my mind settled on—PUJOT. The *Pujot* was everywhere; it was like that lion emblem at the front gave that beige automobile an insatiable urge to roam as though it was in the jungle. I told myself that the painters at *Pujot* assemblies either did not know any other colour apart from beige or there were no other colours. It had a unique purr, one that announced its arrival and said a lot about its departure. I found myself hunting for more and more of *Pujots,* leading me to discover they came in three versions, each design meant for a different category.

The Sedan was a 5-seater, built to be the go-to family car especially for the bourgeoisie class of that time. My research also yielded a weird finding; that 504 sedans were frowned upon near banking halls because they were the preferred getaway cars by bank robbers due to their quick pick-speed. The hatchback was the longer version of the sedan but with so much space inside it easily fit up to 10 people. It was still a family car, but for those that believed in 'filling the world'. It was a favourite for the Flying Squad and *Wepesi.* I never got satisfactory answers why the Flying Squad police unit was always on wheels and not in the air. *Wepesi,* on the other hand, was a public transport service that made good use of the hatchback's resilience, speed, and loading capacity to rake in the business. Every village had someone with a *Wepesi,* so booking was done at their home then the driver went round the village collecting his passengers before the rubber met the tarmac.

The third version was the pick-up truck. It common with the farmers, sawmill owners, and people in the construction industry. Those pick-ups packed to capacity sand, timber, furniture, household goods, glass, and cement, name them. As long as whatever you were to haul found space to squeeze on the carriage, the 504 was good to go. Now, someone looked at all that space and realized that if they closed off the open back it could serve as a public service vehicle. It did. The flat rooftop was fitted with a carrier, serving as a cargo holder for luggage. In the quest to make the most out of the least available space, turn boys made passengers who could did not find space inside to hang at the rear. There would be close to five passengers hanging from one point to the other, making the overloaded truck lean backwards like an aircraft taking off. Continued hanging meant the rear shock absorbers got messed, the pick-up lost original posture and took up the shape of a hyena.

The experience of using those passenger pick-up trucks was exhilarating. Inside, the passengers sat facing each other. The awkward moments when passengers, who were all strangers, sat on opposite benches and had to face each other by force throughout the journey. Before the journey ended you ended asking one another 'where did we meet' and just like that relationships were established. One or two married couples met this way. Innovative capitalist as we are, a smaller bench could be squeezed in the little space between the two main benches and charged as a child seat. The fun with sitting there was that you had the pleasure of looking at fellow passengers at the same time turning backwards to peep through the little window behind and watching how the driver was fumbling with the gears.

I was in Class four when Dad started building a permanent house for us. All those other years we had been hurled up in a semi-permanent square structure with four rooms—the master bedroom, kids' bedroom, kitchenette, and sitting area that doubled up as the dining, recreational and guest lounge. That should give you an idea of how difficult it always was for me to play hide and seek with Thatcher in such a confined space. There was a second semi-permanent structure adjacent to the main house, slightly smaller but with similar sub-divisions. It served as a store, servant's quarters, and sleeping house for our few chicken and one emaciated cow. In a village yet to be connected to the power grid, we made do with lanterns which sometimes ran out of kerosene without notice. Now add to the fact that it is believed that night runners come from there.

I have never seen a night runner, but stories abound of who they were, what time they clocked in and who among their children was being groomed to take over the mantle. Some of the names mentioned were of very respectable members in society like the men of cloth, even community leaders, someone you could not guess. Night runners were said to move around naked in the dark of the night, riding an animal that resembled a leopard, and that they were most active during the full moon night. They disturbed the night—threw stones on people's roofs, scratched doors, farted at people's windows—till almost dawn when they went back to sleep.

Their wives were said to wait for them in the kitchen, their legs perched on the cooking stones as a way of protection otherwise any slight loss of balance meant their husband was nabbed. Upon marriage, some girls got recruited into it but there were those that learnt of the goings-on in the new home and came back to their parents hardly a week after. Those were just not cut out to be accomplices to night running.

One day, I found myself playing with one of the boys rumoured to be from a night running family. I was aware he was a product of a suspected night runner, but kids never know how to discriminate until adults fill their minds with hate and knowledge of whom to hate and why. The play date went well, and he at no point mentioned night running or took me into their barn to introduce me to the family 'leopard.' We played outdoors the whole afternoon until it was time for me to go back home.

"Nimeambiwa umeonekana kwa kina X, ni ukweli?" Mother asked when I got home.

"Ukweli."

"Mama yangu. Woi! Hii ni nini nilizaa?"

Thatcher covered her face with both hands, looking down in despair and shook her head like I had just brought shame to our entire generation.

"*Umeacha* toys *hapa uende kurukaruka uchi na warogi huko nje.* Hillary, *wewe unanitafutia maneno!*"

I felt ashamed of myself too, and the generation that would come after me. I had disgraced a good woman, and a family that was starting to build a great reputation around the neighbourhood for good morals. I could not wrap my mind around Hillary scuttling around the village at night naked in the company riding ghoulish creatures, nor farting at people's windows. I never went back.

Midway through the construction of our new house, Dad ran out of money so it stalled at the lintels. Forlorn brick walls stood in front of the semi-permanent house, like the aftermath of a civil war. All that was visible were gaping window and door spaces as well as green shrubs shooting out of the floor. Patches of green mould clung to the walls, fortified by the just concluded rainy season. Some bricks clipped at the edges, and what had not long before been a mason's haven screamed of loneliness, like a forgotten child in the hallways of an enormous mall. The high mound of sand that once sat beside the structure had long been carried away, leaving behind a small heap on the verge of disappearing under the growing grass.

Naysayers began rumour mongering that some enemy of the Ambani's had gone to a witchdoctor to 'lock' the house. Who would not have believed it anyway as there were cases of individuals who only sunk the foundation, went back to the city and never returned home. Not that they lost their jobs or had financial upheavals, they just erased that project off their minds completely.

The structure became Tope's and my hangout. Every evening after school we would climb to the highest point, sit and watch people go about their businesses. The vantage point afforded us some of the best views of the village, even as far as the local stream where girls met in the evenings to gossip. The view was not exactly breath-taking; just roofs of grass thatched houses and a few iron sheet roofs rotting away after years of braving the rains. We sat there unaware of what we benefitted from that newfound hobby but felt that it filled some void we could not place a finger on.

That would quickly turn out to be the transition we needed from just crushing on girls and writing letters that got intercepted to actually having girls in our lives. It started the evening Tope tapped me on the shoulder and pointed at something in the distance. From our birds' eye view, two girls balanced baskets full of corn on their heads going to the *posho* mill. The *posho* mill was our little taste of Mesopotamia; the thin line between physically grinding corn to flour using stones or milling it with the help of a diesel powered machine. The flour was used to make *ugali,* our staple food. We ate *ugali* with eggs, greens, fermented milk, fish, and occasionally with beef. Most Sundays we ate *githeri*, apart from special days like Christmas or when visitors came over when an unlucky chicken lost its life. You ate that stuff so much you would almost feel corn growing in your stomach. It was like a curse; born to eat *ugali* and die eating *ugali*. The village was a giant *ugali*-eating zone!

Tope had, to my surprise, acquired whistling skills that I was not aware of. He used this newfound talent to get the girls to look our direction. We made some hand signals to which they nodded in approval. We knew them, same way everyone knew everyone else in the village. They lived two compounds away from ours, and though we had seen them grow up, none of us had taken interest in them until this minute. They were twins! They had the same voice, walking style, burst out laughing in the same manner, even had the same sheepish smiles. Only the names were different—Miriam and Keith.

After confirming that Thatcher was not hiding somewhere with a *mwiko* to clobber the mischief out of us, we jumped down from the building and dashed to join the twins. I, to this date, have no idea what we said to the girls on their trip to the *posho* mill, but by the time we got back, we had girlfriends next door. It was almost dark—we had gotten carried away with our quest for girlfriend, which drew Thatcher's attention—and she was waiting for us with a *mwiko.*

"Mmetoka wapi?" she asked no one in particular.

"Kununua wembe."

I have never known where Tope conjured that answer within a fraction of a second since we had not crafted what to say. That meant if Thatcher had made the mistake of separating us and asking a similar set of questions individually we were toast. .

"Woii. Madam Jane *amekuwa maskini siku hizi hata wembe hana. Lazima watoto watoroke polepole waende kujinunulia.* Anne, *nipatie hiyo kiboko."*

Knowing that we had much more to lose by giving contradicting answers, we stuck to the razor blade story and did not add any further details. We had learnt over time that the struggle to validate a lie always created gaping loopholes that Thatcher often exploited to blow cases wide open. Silence would be the code here. The thought of having our first real girlfriends was worth every flogging. She would stop, try to gather fresh information in between the flogging then continue whipping us when nothing was said. She got tired along the way upon realizing she was trying to milk stones. For the first time, she was sure there was something fishy going on and she had no idea what it was. We could almost feel how thick her frustration was.

We retreated to our room and quickly planned the next meeting with the twins. We had gathered that they were in the same class at a different school, a class ahead of Tope, which meant two ahead of me. We could not tell them apart, but reached a gentleman's agreement that Miriam was Tope's while Keith was mine.

Our meetings were awkward because even after so many times together, we still had trouble differentiating them. It was for each vixen to align to her respective boyfriend. Trouble was when you were alone, bumped into both and they decided to keep quiet so that you wallow in confusion. It was even more difficult meeting one alone because you did not know where to start a chat from, just in case you start yapping things meant for the other. The good news is; those vixens were great company. The bad news (or still good depending on how you viewed it) was that none of us ever proposed intimacy. No requests from either side for a kiss, peck, sex, nothing. It was all just sharing information about our different teachers, whom we generally hated, what lessons were challenging, and when the next *posho* mill visit was. That was purest form of love, made in heaven and for four young souls in the village of Maragoli.

When we were not working on the liaison with Miriam and Keith, we sneaked out at night to watch mobile cinema. The green van pulling a black generator would be in Mbale every Tuesday and Saturday night. What had been a bubbling open-air market during the day would quickly be converted into an open auditorium, with the crowd seated on one side and a projector erected on another, beaming moving pictures on a white screen. There was always that one superhero—Van Damme, Jet Li or Rambo—fighting against a generally impenetrable enemy, and still emerging victorious. Typical David versus Goliath case beamed right there in front of our young eyes. The fiction was exhilarating, overly exaggerated—like people fighting mid-air as if the law of gravity was a fallacy, or a human surviving hundreds of gunshots. People like me are so scared of guns that you don't even need to shoot, a shot in the air and I am half-dead such that I'd need a lot of counselling after I come to to assure me that I did not just resurrect. So, watching an individual soak in all those gunshots and still dust himself well enough to exert revenge and triumph mesmerized us.

We started creating scrapbooks with newspaper cuttings of whomever our heroes were. Those that felt inspired learnt those moves and would fight each other for fun or during disagreements. More than once a boy went back home nose-bleeding or with a broken tooth after a Van Damme Vs Jet Li wannabes fought. Accompanying him would be a lie because parents who got wind you were in a fight beat the crap out of you, your bleeding nose notwithstanding. I never fought, largely because I was too slender and soft to withstand the pain; I did better in the cheering squad.

The walk home in the darkness after the film was not without its share of drama. There were no streetlights in Mbale. In that darkness, you could not differentiate your own brother from a patrol cop, nor spot whoever was throwing a rotten egg at you. Man those eggs stunk; I wonder why people threw rotten eggs in your face.

There were no night police patrols in the village, they would only come to arrest a few for bribes. So, the police lay an elaborate ambush and spring it while we were getting back from the cinema. In the chaos that ensued as everyone ran helter-skelter for their dear lives, some got injured; too bad for you if you were arrested, you'd spent the night at the stinking police cells awaiting your parents to come and bribe your way out of the cells. The thought of your parent coming to bail you out with charges like 'drunk and disorderly or in possession of illegal drugs' was mindboggling. If you had an 'evil' parent, he or she would get the news and decide to let you stay behind bars for an extra day, then bail you very early on Monday morning before your name made it to the list of those headed for court.

Before that holiday came to an end, Mom gave us fare to go visit grandma in Chavakali, a 25-minute drive. Visiting grandma was one of the best treats any parent would give their children; grandmas spoilt us, they were the best guys, like a friend behind the enemy lines. Moreover, grandmothers always prayed for you, special and honest prayers for you to prosper in life and be great.

The moment grandma saw you from a distance, she would run towards you with arms wide open, gather you into herself like a chicken protecting its chicks from a hawk. In her arms you felt how happy she was you visited, all her happiness wrapped with you in the embrace.

Where I come from, you can tell how much of a treasured guest you are depending on whether or not the family will go to the trouble of slaughtering a fowl for you. Grandma did not need to think twice about being bereft of a bird for you. She would call out whoever was around and point at the day's victim, then the chase to have it caught and slaughtered began. We ran after the birds with gusto, turbo-charged, through banana plantations, maize, cassava fields, and sometimes across rivers! You did not think of anything else as you chased it, just imagination of roasting and munching it. Often, as the chase intensified, you got volunteers who joined in to help catch the fowl, an unwritten law that required joining the chase regardless of whether or not you will get a piece. Both the fowl and the crowd ran for a purpose, like a mob justice crowd trying to rid the streets of a suspected thief, and the suspect hoping to live yet another day. The goal was one—the chicken, and there was no giving up the chase.

To reinforce how much valued you were as a guest, grandma would not only fry the first bird specifically for you but also give you another live one to take back home with you. You were to secure it tightly on your lap, its head facing behind, as it was believed that a chicken which saw directions easily found its way back. The instruction on the live bird was that not even your father, however authoritative or 'difficult' he was, had a say over it. It had to be raised to adulthood, and if it was to be slaughtered for whatever reason, the family had to humbly seek permission from you.

On days when the visit lasted longer, grandma set up a quick lodge for you, a foldable spring bed that only appeared whenever you needed to sleep and was folded back into a small heap in the morning then tucked under another bed. The problem with the foldable bed was that the springs were generally loose, so much that when you jumped into bed you sort of sunk in the middle like a disappointing soufflé. The danger was that if one of the springs snapped, you and your one-inch mattress crashed to the floor in the middle of the night. You would wake up angry that your sweet dream was rudely disrupted, coupled with the thought that you had to gather the bed back together.

Most of us were perennial bed-wetters. We would sleep dry and wake up wet without a clue when and how that had happened. When morning came we had to start with what we hated most—carrying out the drenched bedding to air under the sun. It was a usual sight to walk into any compound and be met by a line of mattresses leaning against the fence or lying on the grass in the open. Because that chore was humiliating, we played dumb and left the wet bedding indoors. In the evening, when you realized you had to sleep, in the very wet bed, that you hated yourself.

There was this theory peddled around that to stop a kid from wetting the bed, a snake had to be killed and tied round his or her waist for one night. I bet whoever came up with that myth knew most people would be found dead tying a dead snake around their child's waist, forget hunting for a live one to kill. Most parents therefore resigned to fate and waited for the day the kid would grow out of it.

CHAPTER 8

OF CHRISTMAS AND OPENING DAYS

ON 7TH DECEMBER, 1994, my last born sister, Juliet, was born. I bet my folks had planned for her to share a birthday with Jesus Christ but she chose to pop out earlier. The only mistake was that they had forgotten to prepare us psychologically to expect an ever-wailing addition to the family, and in our naivety we had also missed Thatcher's bigger than normal tummy. We watched in awe as Thatcher bathed the 15-centimeter creature looking like a piglet, with curly hair and toes the size of a watch battery.

The new addition came with a lot of tears. She would cry when she wanted to sleep, cry when she woke up, cry to breastfeed, cry during that feeding, cry because someone else—other than Thatcher—carried her, and cried to poop. We put up with a lot of crying and poop that Christmas season. Everywhere you turned there was either milk, a nappy, or baby clothes. A whole shelf in the family cupboard was set aside for bottles, medicine, and Gripe Water.

The child came with both good and bad news. Bad news first: we would not spend our holiday in Nairobi like had been the norm, which meant that Dad would be the one to travel to the village. We did not even know how people spent all that time in the village until January, especially with a crying baby. The good news was that Mom had something to fully engage her ever-prying mind, which translated to us having all the time for our twins!

Being in the village during Christmas also allowed us to witness a strange ritual that we had never witnessed—*kufukuza madimoni* (chasing away evil spirits). During the ritual, people converged at night, everyone carrying whatever household utensil they could lay their hands on, then the crowd would beat the Hell out of those utensils, turning the village into a frenzy in what was believed to drive the spirits of death, divorce, hunger, and witchcraft that had dogged that year. I found it idiotic because our village never seemed to run out of the above even after chasing them year in and out.

"Sasa wanafukuza hiyo madimoni iende wapi?" I once asked.

"Wanaifukuza iende huko Lake Victoria," I was told.

Holy Mary mother of Jesus! That same lake that provided us with the fish we devoured on days Thatcher woke up with God's grace. My attempts to delve into the depths of that story were futile, I had to resign to the fact that I had, to that point, already eaten a lot of evil spirits. These people did not know just how much of a dilemma they had put me in, because I now had to decide whether to let go of my beloved fish dishes or resign ingesting demons. I bet you can rightly guess what I chose.

Tope and I also decided to be adventurous and join the group of boys and girls in our church practicing the Christmas carols. A select few rehearsed to represent our church on Christmas day at an inter-church competition. The rest were there to run away from chores and noise back home (like us) or hunt for boy/girlfriends. We were lucky to have had acquired the twins before the 'gold rush' began, so we were sorted on that front. Since we had spent most of our holiday following our girls up and down the village like a puppy, we had missed lots of practice and rehearsal time, which nullified any chance may have had of joining the church band. Again, even if we were by some miracle allowed to, that would have been the beginning of losing vital points for our church because we had very bad non-musical voices.

It was still a great discovery, a break from baby poop and the twins. We were at the church gate every evening until Christmas day you would have thought we were seasoned choir members.

Christmas day controlled the month of December. On that day, people that didn't know their own birthdays celebrated the birth of some Jewish boy born many years ago. On that day, ninety percent of households ate chicken, rice, and chapatti in the same sitting. Under normal circumstances, those dishes were spread across the year and taken individually.

Mama Zuena was the village chapatti expert. Once upon a time, one of our Protestant neighbours got tired of idling in the village taking *chang'aa* and getting arrested, so he went to Mombasa to seek employment. The family did not hear from him for so many years, and since we did not have Internet, mobile phones, or social media, everyone forgot him. The few people who went to Mombasa came back with conflicting stories; some saying he had been spotted loading luggage at the port, others that he had been married by a very old Italian woman with a palace somewhere in Nyali, but the most recurrent tale was that he had converted to Islam and even become an imam. One day, out of the blue, the neighbour, now in his prime, alighted from a Coast Bus at the town dressed in a white kanzu. He had a disgusting long goatee, in tow a light-complexioned female dressed in night-black *buibui* and *niqab*. Two kids, a boy and girl, scuttled behind them. Mama Zuena and the two Muslim kids became a fixture in the village. Since she did not celebrate Christmas, she was sought after by households to make chapattis for them on Christmas. I see chapattis being rolled and cooked by dusty roadsides at grimy streets in Nairobi and fail to understand how we mutilated this delicacy that held prestige for eons.

It is interesting how even your favourite food, once you've devoured it, sates you to the point of not wanting any more. The moment we got full, Christmas was done. By sundown, January beckoned. It was as if days jumped from 26th December to 31st then school opening day. The prayer on every school-going child was that our then philanthropic president would come through like he always did and postpone the school opening for a week. That was the time even those who had zero interest in radio religiously listened to every news bulletin to hear one sentence:

'Mtukufu Rais Daniel Toroitich Arap Moi, hivi leo ameamru kuahirishwa kwa siku ya kufungua shule hadi juma lijalo tarehe . . .'

He decided that he would not extend this particular holiday we had enjoyed more than the rest. We listened, and listened, and listened, even to the obituary announcements just in case that important piece of news had been overlooked in the main bulletin. Nothing. School year of 1995 was as per the date given during closing.

Opening day in January was hated and loved in equal measure. First, the grass would have grown so high in and around the school compound and classrooms reeked of the wild. The same desks people had tossed around carelessly on closing day needed to be arranged, and this time they packed dust with all its ancestors. To restore normalcy and bring the school back to conducive learning environment, we spent the opening day cleaning, dusting, trimming hedges, arranging furniture, and sorting books. At the end of it, we would officially be allowed to occupy the next step in the curriculum, leaving our former classrooms behind with all the memories and experiences of the previous year.

Column 1was the first one you came across as you walked in through the classroom door; where the bright pupils sat, the one who was position one being at the front. It was like the genius zone. Column 2 had the average pupils while Row 3 was where no parent wants his or her child to be. It was a sort of segregation, brains on one side, those believed to be slow on the other, far away from the brains as if stupidity was contagious. The weird bit was that Column 3 had more boys than girls, which was by all means a bad sign; that mothers in my area were giving birth to not so bright boys. This story always had a sad ending. The boys on Column 3 hardly made it past high school. Every time I drive into Mbale, I see them perched on motorbikes at the bus stage soliciting for passengers. It is as if that row condemned them to a life of failure, like being there was a sign you were in school to keep you from getting into village trouble; stealing, smoking, or impregnating young girls. Sometimes a slow child needs to be mixed up with bright ones so that they offer some hope and a different look at life.

Settling in the new classroom opened doors to a whole year ahead, complete with new learning points, new assignments, new teachers, and new punishments for new misdemeanours. It meant knowing who had repeated the previous class, who had moved schools, who had transferred from another school, who your new desk mate would be. The only good thing about opening day in January was that everyone had a story of how they had spent their Christmas, so if you took time to listen to each of your classmates, you had quite a lot of infotainment the whole day. Not all of these stories were true though, every class had its own pathological liars who would cook stories to the best the others. All you had to do was listen and note the loopholes in their stories. It was wise to keep quiet even if you knew from the onset that you were being lied to because most liars had a temper and hated being questioned over their stories. No one wanted to create an enemy when the year was that young.

Hussein, the only classmate who had been to Mombasa, had the most interesting stories straight out of Majengo King'orani, from seeing a jinni woman with goat hooves and to mermaids asking people to go play with them in the Indian Ocean. He would warn us of how in Mombasa people don't just pluck leaves or pick anything from the road because djinns came in form of anything, including money. He mentioned how someone had picked a 50-shilling note then it started asking him why he was carrying what did not belong to him. The scariest of them all was being told of children who would sleep in their beds only to wake up and find themselves perched on top of a palm tree. None of us had been to Mombasa so there was no way to authenticate the stories.

I noticed that Nebert Injenga looked aloof on this particular day. Most of us were nursing opening day hangovers, yes, but we didn't hide in one corner of the class curled up like a brooding chicken. Being the good friend, I went to check up on him—he looked chubbier than usual, and his lower jaw was protruding out of his mouth. I had not even started my inquiry before Norega sounded an alarm:

"Hillary, *shauri yako!*" Any time someone said *shauri yako* to me I knew better than to continue with what I was doing.

"Injenga ave nizindendeyi!" she replied. "And mumps is contagious."

In a flash, all the desks near Injenga were empty, with everyone scampering for safety, even if it meant squeezing on an already full desk. Half of Column 1 was deserted.

Nebert was evidently in a lot of pain, but we were warned to keep distance lest we looked like him. Fanice, I believe her other name was Mmboga, offered the first hopeful solution to the boy—he had to look for a tree called Mutembe, pick a bunch of firewood then run around it ten times singing *"Izindendeyi hera kumutembe"* (Mumps, please remain on the Mutembe tree). He would then have to throw the bunch of firewood on the tree and take off at high speed, never looking back. That is how he would get healed. The only Mutembe tree all of us knew was in Mbale town, next to a church called Friends. A bit of normalcy was restored when Mr Lodenyo walked into class and asked Nebert to go back home and come back when completely healed, leaving behind fears that those who had moved close to him would be the next victims.

No one else in our class went down with mumps.

A lot of the village myths and general beliefs were woven to explain the mystery of illnesses and death, long before a lot of sicknesses could be diagnosed and treated in hospital. Witchcraft and the 'bad eye' are deeply entrenched in the mind of the villager.

Baby Juliet had, on this day, been crying since morning, and Mom could not understand what the problem was. She took her to hospital but came back with a very weak diagnosis, like the paediatrician simply decided not to tell her she could not find any sensible ailment. Our then house help, Mama Levi, who had raised seven children herself and helped many mothers around give birth, took a keen look at Juliet's body and came up with a diagnosis. Mama Levi needed no scanning machine, blood samples, or stool to know that someone had looked at Juliet with bad eyes.

In the village, there were women believed they had 'bad eyes' so lethal that they just need to look at you for a second and you fell sick, had an accident, or failed in your endeavour. It was said that they could even make animals sick, especially calves and lambs. The psychology behind it is that they looked at things and got jealous, and in what no one can explain, this jealousy caused the human or animal in question to face some misfortune. Just like the night runners, everyone knew these women, so whenever you saw them walk into your compound, someone would be asked to quickly hide the baby and lock up the cattle.

At that point, Thatcher and Mama Levi started going through the list of everyone who had visited our compound or set eyes on Juliet in the last two days. They vetted the names and soon had a prime suspect who was rumoured to have bad eyes but not yet confirmed. It looked like the rumour had been true all along yet Mom had let her guard down not only allowing her to visit but also hold the baby.

Sickness as a result of 'bad eyes' was not treated with modern medicine, only herbs worked. I was immediately sent to go get Aireni (our pronunciation for Irene) as soon as possible. Aireni was always hunting for or moving around with herbs to administer to victims of bad eyes. I found her at the front yard of her house, leaves in her hand, most probably preparing a drug for another victim. Since she and Mom were very 'tight', she decided to forego that earlier SOS call and rushed to save 'madam's daughter' with the very leaves she was holding. She may have been way older than me and ageing, but I found it hard trying to keep up with her pace.

She ordered Mama Levi to boil hot water while she chewed the leaves then spat out the juice on Juliet's little stomach. I watched from a distance as Airen, with the precision of a professional medicine-woman, administer lifesaving aid on the crying baby. When the hot water arrived in a basin, she immersed another bunch of leaves then washed Juliet in the now green liquid. Soon as she was dried and wrapped in a shawl, she stopped crying and fell asleep, a feat Thatcher and Mama Levi had failed to achieve the whole day. It was like the magic TV show called *Kiini Macho* we watched on days we were allowed.

Immediately the baby slumbered, a kettle brimming with hot tea was pushed before Airen. That was like a 'thank you note' before payment was discussed. Apart from *ugali*, my people have affinity for tea. It is like we are cursed for tea. Every household has this big mug called *irikabuuru/irisuvira*, one that can accommodate two litres of tea at a go. They mostly come in plastic and metal, and a Luhyia brother or sister will empty it in one sitting and walk away as though they had not drank two litres of tea. Plastic is preferred because we do not really know how to wait for tea to cool, we take it hot as it hits the table, and plastic does not burn the lips. The other problem with a metallic mug is that its surfaces chip with time due to scratches and overheating, which usually gives it a bad old look.

Households do not usually have very many of these mugs otherwise the tea would never be enough for all. The mugs are not given to visitors, only small melamine ones that see the light of the day on such occasions. Drinks are served in intervals of forty-five minutes to one hour: soda, tea, soda, in that order. Time for meals is time to talk as well, and talk loudly, while asking fellows to pass you the soup, salt, or bowl of food. We don't take our beloved *ugali* at many a event, preferring to substitute it with rice or chapatti because those are rare. We do not get sated, we just get tired, or are reminded by a concerned party that it is time to stop eating. Foods like spaghetti and pasta have no space on our tables, they are too light for our stomachs. When people go for an event, by the time they head home look like they are seven months pregnant, some can't even breathe well. Surprisingly, we overfeed yet remain petit.

This is taught at an early age. Every time you attend an event, your mother is quick to point out that she will be too tired to go home and prepare supper again after a long day at the event, so everybody has to eat enough to last up to the next day. That is when you find even little children giving adults a run for their money on that table. On a good day, the food remains and we ask for it to be packed in plastic bags so that we continue the eating spree at our homes. A good host will pack different meals in different bags so that it is easy to separate them when you get home, the 'evil' one will pack rice together with chicken stew, chapatti, beef and *mandazi* in one bag. Sharp hosts usually feed their family before the guests arrive, or keep away a part of the food to eat later. Failure to do so they risk of having guests who will devour and carry everything leaving them with nothing. Mom would tell us to eat to our fill early in the day rather than wait because she knew we would go around staring at her visitors with emaciated looks, eyes following their hands from plate to mouth like hyenas.

CHAPTER 9

THE NEXT LEVEL MISDEMEANOURS

DAD'S NEW HOUSE was completed around August of 1995. Thatcher, Dad, and my sisters migrated to the new house, while Tope and I were left with what had been the family house. Humphrey, the garden boy, kept the other house. This ushered in a new era into our lives. It started harmlessly by Humphrey joining us at our house at night to while the night away before we started dozing then he would go back to his bed. In a way, none of us had anticipated the experience, we crossed into territory that was both scary and exciting. The idea came forth one night when Humphrey informed us that during one of his daily farm visits, he bumped into an unidentified pile of chicken eggs hidden in a bush. None of our brooding chicken was missing eggs, so we could tell they were eggs from a stray chicken. Such a discovery should not make any primary school boy excited, but somehow that news was exhilarating. We decided to keep a keen eye and find out which chicken was laying them. The plan was that if the were eggs from one of our chicken, we would carry them to safety and give her a better nest inside the house.

When a week went by without any sign of a chicken laying them or a neighbour asking about missing eggs, Humphrey carried them home. We had our usual pre-sleep meeting and unanimously agreed to cook and eat them, just the three of us as the rest of the family snored the night away. Half were spoilt, meaning they had been lying out there for a while. We had already had supper, and were by all means not hungry, but somehow the thought of digging into a bunch of stray eggs was lucrative. They were the most delicious eggs we had ever eaten.

For the first time, we discovered what we had been missing all along—something illegal to keep us busy at night. From that night onwards, 'Part 2', as we called it, would be mandatory before we slept. It meant that we would have supper with the rest, eat just a little to pass the meal, wait for everybody else to sleep then cook our 'Part 2'. This was to be a top secret, just for the three. It was not hunger which made us look forward to 'Part 2' but the knowledge that we were in a way rebelling against an oppressive regime and getting away with it.

Since Tope and I had no source of income, Humphrey accepted to donate ten percent of his salary every month to the Part 2 kitty. It was like tithe, and he did religiously. We soon had our own salt, sugar, Blue Band margarine, cooking oil, and tealeaves. Every time Humphrey got the chance to go to Mbale, he came back with a stash of *omena* for our stock. The one unbelievable bit in this arrangement is that as much as we were in charge of the cows, which were three by now, we handled all the milk and it never even once occurred to us to sell part of that milk behind Mom's back to add onto our kitty. We declared all the milk we got and gave out all the cash from sales.

Within a very short period, Part 2 grew in leaps and bounds. The operation traversed all available boundaries. Our next big mission was in line—avenging a lost chicken. This chicken vendetta started one day when, during the routine evening head count for the chicken, it was discovered that one was missing. A mature chicken doesn't just disappear in my village. If it is a 'new' chicken, meaning it had come into the compound recently, then there is always the second option that it strayed and forgot its way home, so it was either in some bush or with a different flock in the neighbourhood, but not a chicken that had been in that compound for ages. Someone had made away with it. No two ways about it.

We set out on the boring task of knocking doors and asking about the missing chicken. 'None' of the neighbours had seen it. We were almost giving up the search and heading back home when Humphrey's eyes caught what looked like feathers in one of our neighbour's backyard. We moved closer to inspect, and all were in agreement that those were feathers from our missing chicken. Evidence had been found, so it was a closed case that the chicken was never going to be found. Mom shouted about it for all neighbours to hear, without pointing fingers or mentioning anyone then left the rest to God as she always did.

I have never known why the loss of that chicken cut us deep that much, but we made a decision the same night that Humphrey, Tope, and I were going to avenge on behalf of the family. The twist was that the rest of the family, including Mom, was not supposed to know. The thought of a neighbour eating chicken that was out of bounds for us did not sit well with us.

That chicken mission came when we were planning our greatest heist yet, setting us a day back because we had had to waste valuable time following up on a chicken and plotting revenge. This heist was to burglarize one of the most guarded compounds in the village, not to steal anything valuable really but ripe bananas! There were bananas in the main house that day, but these particular ones looked (and probably tasted) better.

We all knew we were toying with death, but the adrenaline that came with it made the urge irresistible. We had gotten away with several escapades and, with each successful one, we kept getting better. We learned from past mistakes, tried out new skills, came up with several ways of doing things, and most importantly believed in ourselves. We broke our own records and set the bar higher every day. We expanded the area, the options grew, and the number of frustrated neighbours increased.

At 18 years, Humphrey was the eldest in our cartel but he was the muscle while Tope and I were the brains. We were barely 14 years old.

On this particular night, Humphrey's height was of utmost importance. We assigned him the role of lifting me on his shoulders, high enough for me to reach the bananas then as I cut them piece-by-piece, while Tope would be on the ground collecting the loot.

Balanced on Humphrey's shoulders, I extended my hands to reach for the bunch. Something crackled. It wasn't the banana leaves. I hesitated. Deathly silence descend on us. Humphrey and Tope were quiet as well, like they too had heard the crackle. Operating in pitch darkness without communication is not easy. You have to assume that the other parties are in tandem, and that if anything goes wrong they will be quick to react and find the escape route.

The only undoing with getting away with crime is that after a while you forget the ever-imminent danger of being caught, so when you plan things you forget to add a 'what if' or 'in the event of' clause. That is how seasoned criminals get arrested.

That is when I saw it—a lanky human silhouette tiptoed towards us, carrying something menacing in its hand. I did not make out what it was, but in my village people don't go out investigating disturbances at night carrying simple tools, we go armed for war—machetes, garden rakes, hammers, spears, clubs, any crude weapon you can lay your hands on, not because you are a fierce fighter who will turn the heat on the culprit but to intimidate. It usually works, otherwise if you encounter an unrelenting opponent you become the hunted.

In a split second, I got off Humphrey's shoulder and hit the ground with a thud. I saw a million stars, and my life flashed right before my eyes, all the things I would miss—girls and 'Part2'. I guess if I went to heaven that minute, God would not have looked at me, He would have simply ushered me to the other side, the one with burning fire. I shook my head just to be sure I was not in transit to heaven.

There was a sharp pain in my left leg though it was manageable, so I ran. Tope and Humphrey were nowhere to be seen, and I could not figure out which direction I was heading. I could still hear footsteps scurrying behind me hard against the earth's crust. I ran as fast as I could and managed to get away. Since I had seen Caterpillars working on the road, I knew there were trenches on both sides, sunk to channel rainwater from the road. I immediately knew the plan—I would jump into one of the trenches then crawl all along up to somewhere I was safe, then I would raise myself back to the road and do the final dash home.

I found myself at the bottom of the trench, with my bottom sunk into something mushy. I hoped it was not what I thought it was. But it was! My nose confirmed. I was sitting on someone's shit, so foul that I almost suffocated. I sat for a few minutes, which felt like hours, analysing the situation to come up with the best course of action to get away. The stench was even affecting my decision making, so I closed my eyes and pulled my trouser down, remaining in underwear. So I was there in the trench, in my underwear, crawling on my bare knees to safety. I finally got to a culvert and knew it was time to get out of that trench and make the sprint home.

Sometimes I wonder what would have happened if in that dash someone got hold of me in my briefs, in the middle of the night. News would have spread by morning that Madam Jane's son, the one and only Lisimba, was a night runner.

I managed to get home undetected. Humphrey was already there, lights off. I could see the sigh of relief on his face when he opened the door and saw me, but he was also looking at the lower part of me that was naked.

"Suruali imeenda wapi?" he asked.

I told him to let me in first then I would tell him what had happened. We put the lights back on, and for minutes few words were exchanged. Tope was not yet back, partly because he could have been caught by the night patrol cops shouting our names and describing the failed mission, and partly because I was back half-naked. Our faces brightened when we answered the knock on the door and it was Tope standing there, alone. We held a crisis meeting and struck the bananas off our list. We decided to turn our energies back home to avenging our stolen chicken.

I remember passing on the same road on my way to school and peeping to see my soiled trouser in the trench, a piece of history I hated to be associated with. It rained that evening, washing away all the inequities we had perpetuated the previous night. The rainwater even carried away the evidence.

Karma is a bitch! A few days later, the neighbour's chicken came to our compound. Part of the previous night's *ugali* had been broken down into little pieces and spread at the corner of our veranda so that when our chicken were let out, they would converge there for their morning meal. Avulole, the suspect neighbour's latest chicken, was however earlier than our own. We momentarily dropped all preparations for school and surrounded Avulole, everyone positioned strategically to make this as short and smooth a chase as possible.

The capture went as planned. In less than two minutes, we had Avulole in Humphrey's hands, headed to the hiding room where she would stay under the cover of a basket until her time came that night.

Fried chicken with an accompaniment like *ugali* or rice is delicious. Fried chicken eaten plain without an accompaniment is wonderful. Now imagine fried chicken, acquired illegally, prepared as revenge and eaten plain as 'Part 2'. It was sumptuousness on a different level!

Whenever Tope and I talk about these escapades, we conclude that it is the pressure from all corners in our lives that turned us into great thinkers. The problem was that no one noticed our great minds and thought of tapping into them, that is why we channelled them into mischief. Good thing with us was that we were generally well-behaved in school, always top of our classes, and carried ourselves around with respect so you could not really read through the rotten underbelly by just looking at us.

CHAPTER 10

RIGHT PLACE, WRONG TIME

WITH TOPE AND I in one house and Humphrey in the other, it was difficult communicating especially in the morning when we wanted to wake each other up. With mobile phones being a foreign phenomenon then, we remembered the basic telephone technology science had taught in school. It was simple: a tin on one side, another tin on the other, a cord in between them. Surprisingly, the gadget could transmit information from one tin to the other.

The tin telephone between our two houses would not have worked because the real need for it was to wake up someone from sleep, unless one of us slept with the tin on his ear. We decided to keep the idea of the cord from one house to the other, but the tins at the end would have to be replaced with something more aggressive, something that was noisy enough to jolt someone out of sleep. Only one thing seemed to suffice—bottle tops. We played with homemade shakers; all you needed was a tree branch in the shape of a Y, tie a cord between the two tips then run it through flattened bottle tops and you had your toy.

But there was a problem: soda was a luxury that we rarely enjoyed. You needed at least ten bottle tops on each shaker for the idea to work. We could only get the bottle tops at the local pub. Now, we may have developed runaway traits over an extended period, but alcohol had not joined them yet. We did not bother with alcohol mainly because it was a very obvious form of rebellion among children our age, and we didn't believe in going the direction everyone else did. But this once we had to get bottle tops from the pub, meaning one or all of us had to go to a pub. I volunteered.

It was a simple assignment, or so I thought—walk into the pub, go straight to the counter and request whoever was there to collect some of those they had opened from people's beer bottles that day, get out. I had the misfortune of meeting the slowest waitress in Maragoli. She listened to my request, said yes then started dragging her feet around. She would go to serve a drink on one table, collect cash on another, and disappear through some door leading to a room that headed to who-knows-where then reappear after a few minutes. All this time I stood at the counter of the pub in a village where Mom was a well-known figure.

I was not always courting trouble, it is trouble that was forever stalking me like a hungry panther. The neighbour from across the road from our compound walked in. He seemed pleasantly surprised as he joined me at the counter to order some mediocre liquor called Kibuku. He stood there silently staring at me with his big popping eyes. I kept quiet too. His Kibuku was handed over to him through the rails at the counter, then the waitress asked me to follow her to the back of the pub where they kept the garbage.

"Help yourself," the waitress told me.

I only needed twenty bottle tops but they were so many I ended up collecting about fifty and left. I do not know whether that was just greed or corruption building up in me.

Back at home, we quickly got down to developing our prototype. After an hour we started testing it. The first hiccup was that the fibre rope we had used did not have enough tension to shake the bottle tops vigorously enough to generate noise that could wake up people who loved their sleep. We held another crisis meeting. The best cord would be the type we saw on rolls at a Kenya Power tent, the same ones that were being fixed on electric poles to supply power around. But those ones were heavily guarded because another set of mischievous but creative boys stole and used them to make wire toy cars, and none of us was about to get into another dangerous stealing mission after the last one's débâcles. We settled on barbed wire, at least that we could cut from our very own fence with a set of pliers.

Waking each other up had never been easier. Whoever woke up earlier just pulled the cord from his side repeatedly, prompting the shaker on the other end to respond with bottle tops hitting on each other. It did not take a week before I was in the dock again, facing Judge Thatcher to answer to charges of being spotted in a pub buying alcohol. There were two counts of felony that I needed to respond to, and my request to get my two lawyers (Tope and Humphrey) was denied.

Question one was when I started drinking, how I had been introduced to it and by whom. I denied that first count.

Question two was where I was getting money to afford bottles of beer at the local pub if I was not stealing her money. That too I denied.

I was found guilty on both counts and sentenced to so many strokes of the cane that I stopped counting.

CHAPTER 11

CLATTER AND CLANG

I AM OF the era that thrived on hand-me-downs. It was a practice which ensured that cloths that elder siblings outgrew did not go to waste. The only problem was that they were mended and patched till they were a mosaic of patchwork, and when they couldn't be patched anymore, they were stashed in pockets and turned into pillows. It is only when the pillows ran out of thickness that these pieces had their final resting place as floor mops or dog bedding.

I had issues with hand-me-downs. One, the shirt or trouser was twice your size, so you basically swam in it, but then you would be told to "grow in it". In most cases, you would never grow fast enough to fit in it, but by then the 'new owner' in line would be pestering you to hand it down. Even panties were handed down, so it was a common occurrence to see girls clutching at their dresses whenever they stood up to hold in place the oversize pantie inside threatening to drop. They played *kati* while holding the panties in place, ran around with the hand still at the waist, only resting from that chore when they sat down. During P.E (Physical Education) lessons or games time, some would get lost in the jumping and forget to safeguard that little piece of treasure.

"*Nyama nyama nyama nyama!*"

"*Nyamaaa!*"

"*Ya ng'ombe*"

"*Nyamaaa!*"

Then the pantie would drop while she was mid-air, falling to the ground before she herself got there. She would hurriedly squat, followed by rushed attempts to pull it back up.

The biggest undoing of school in the village was the lack of amenities. First, schools had a budget to buy food for the teachers, but in this allocation firewood was always left out, so the male students had to carry a piece from home every afternoon when coming back from lunch. It was a punishable offence not to go with firewood; sort of you had a ploy to starve those teachers who toiled every day to impart knowledge on you. It was an obnoxious rule because some families were genuinely poor and didn't even have firewood themselves, depending solely on dried branches that were picked from trees and other branches around the village. 'Proper' firewood was not cheap, a small bunch of five pieces could go up to twenty shillings, which was a lot of money by the standards those days.

The female students on their part carried cow dung. Cow dung is not wasted in the village, it is used as manure, it can be dried and used like charcoal, or smearing on mud floors to rid them of dust. In most schools, lower primary classrooms were not cemented, so the cow dung helped protect our younger brothers and sisters from jiggers. Well, it never worked, though. I've had jiggers. Tope has had jiggers. My sisters have had jiggers. Everyone had jiggers. We pulled the jiggers out using a safety pin then tried to be more hygienic, but there were some who got the bug and it never left their homes. I know of a family which had jiggers so heavily they were spread across from the man of the house to the still suckling babies. They couldn't even walk well; they moved on their heels with their damaged toes pointing upwards. I think it made the pain bearable. It was not a good sight. The family had a daughter in her teens, and save for her moving around on her heels, she was beautiful, yet not a single boy ever thought of approaching her and courting the idea of making her his wife. The family would be branded the jigger family. For instance, if you were talking about a Betty, the other person would ask, "which Betty?", then for clarity the other would respond, "Betty *wa* jiggers".

All classrooms had wooden windows, you either had to close them and stay in darkened classes or open them and brave for harsh weather. The only good thing about the open windows was that it was very easy to tactfully, when the teacher was facing the blackboard, jump out of the class if things got out of hand without the teacher noticing. Things didn't even have to heat up for one to jump out; sometimes it was just because of boredom or hunger. Boyi, 'boy' in Luhyia, was Mama Safi's son. His jumping escapades were because his mother kept away tea or food meant for teachers for him and pass it to him through the back window. When he felt the slightest pang of hunger or thirst, he jumped out, only to reappear looking like an overfed puppy. I am yet to understand why they called her Mama Safi, and it is not like Boyi had a brother or sister called Safi.

During the rainy season when it was storming and harsh, winds blew from all angles, all the windows would be closed, and since the school was yet to be connected to the electricity grid, everyone would be in darkness. The girls, fearing for I don't know what, would huddle in one corner of the room away from the boys. The teachers too would be locked in the staffroom.

So, everyone sat at whatever point of school they were and listened as the strong winds threatened to tear into the badly affixed iron sheets. It is on such occasions that the poem *'Helter skelter, the wind blows the trees away . . .'* rung in our minds, especially that part of *'the roof tops clatter and clang'.* Usually, it would begin with excitement, then fear kicked in as the light faded away and heavy torrents pounded from every corner of the heavens. The longer it took, the angrier we got because no school head in their right mind would dismiss students to go home when it was still raining, so it would mean being released from school later than usual. When it subsided and we were allowed to leave, we would wade and play through all the stagnant water on the way home, to another beating from the parents.

One seemingly normal evening, it started drizzling in slow drops then gained momentum and soon there were torrents hitting our roof as though the Armageddon had come. The expectation was the same; it will do this then subside after a while and finally come to a complete stop. It didn't. The rain went on and on, accompanied by waves of wind that seemed to be on a mission to topple our class over. It was scary, even the brave ones who would normally go around the class tormenting those hiding kept quiet at this one. I guess everyone was imagining the apocalypse.

A flash of lightning struck, followed by a heavy roar of thunder that reverberated through every part of the school. The angry gush of wind brushed on our roof and windows one last time, and, as if on cue, another roar of thunder sounded. There was a loud bang, followed by screams. Abruptly, the rain stopped, and the air was rent with piercing screams. Everyone rushed out of the class to go investigate.

One of the trees near the classrooms had fallen on the Class 4 Block with pupils locked inside.

None of us had any first aid skills. The few scouts our school boasted of only knew how to hoist the flag and lead us in reciting *The Loyalty Pledge*. Moreover, something like that had never happened to our school thus there were no first aid kits. The teachers were grossly underpaid and banks did not give loans easily, so none had a bicycle let alone a car. Mr Lodenyo swung into action, breaking the door after which students poured out of that classroom like a gigantic wave. Some of them screamed "Martha!"

Martha, the perennial number one of the class, was on the floor gasping for breath. There was no evidence of a cut or bruise, but the way she lay there quietly was shocking. The deputy head teacher, who had also joined the rescue mission, looked confused, because Martha's mom was one of those parents who didn't shy away from walking to school any time and hurling obscenities at teachers whenever she felt wronged. The last time we had seen her shout was because each student was asked pay some cash to boost the games kitty because our team had done well and qualified to represent the school at the provincials' level.

I, however, believe his bewildered look was due to the fact that when parents let their children come to your school, they expect you at the helm to be responsible for their safety until they get back home. No parent would be calm when being told that 'it rained, a tree fell and we lost your daughter'.

After resuscitative efforts by Mr Lodenyo, who I was not even sure knew what he was doing, Martha came to. She looked dishevelled but alive. The following week an official announcement was made on assembly that every parent needed to contribute for the school to buy and stock first aid kits. Martha's mom came to school to complain again.

CHAPTER 12

DREAMS MADE, DREAMS KILLED

IN AN AREA with no success stories, the rise of Jackline Kamonya from a nobody to a huge success story was news that spread faster than the president re-shuffling his cabinet. The then president would let you go to work in your chauffeured black Mercedes Benz, send you for a meeting then fire you while you are busy discussing KANU policies in there. You would walk out of your meeting and your official car plus the driver would be gone, off to pick the unknown guy from a farm somewhere who had taken over your position.

Kamonya's fame grew overnight. She was the pride of my people. Our very own nanny believed that Kamonya's grandmother had some sort of close relationship with the lady whose sister gave birth to Kamonya. A very complicated family tree, sort of a spider's web that connected her and that rising star on black and white TV screens every evening. The narrative was that Kamonya had innocently recited a poem to the president, who fell in love with it so much that he had his Personal Assistant call Broadcasting House and order that the day's news anchor be replaced with her . . . and just like that, a teenage star was made.

She embodied hope, a success story that came against the tide, and in an era where only one or two women made it to the airwaves; the late Anne Ofula and Zipporah someone, I forget the second name. I watched Kamonya, the dark skin beauty, stare into my eyes from the other side of the TV reading news. It was then that I knew media and I had were an item. I was not very good looking though, so probably behind the scenes would do well, but either way my career slowly started taking shape because of that now successful woman from my village. She was the first grass to grace real life representation I came across, an epitome of possibility.

Apart from Kamonya, there was *Tausi,* a television drama series of the future. The characters seemed real, the storyline complex and well-scripted. The late Ashina Kibibi had teamed up with one of Kenya's greatest TV producers, Mr Kibwana Onguso, to light up our screens with this real life drama series. You lived the characters, especially Lindi the star of whom you felt like you too were on the streets going through hell while grieving a departed mother and adapt to the life of an urchin. You watched Siti fall head over heels in love with Mjuba and wished it was you. Even Karumanzira (the late Richard Langat) played the witchdoctor role pretty well, to think he was just a random employee at the Nairobi City Council fire brigade unit who had not attended any witchcraft lessons!

While Kamonya and Team Tausi ruled TV, Leonard Mambo Mbotela, Jack Oyoo Silvester, and the late Billy Omala ruled the Swahili radio waves. English was left for John Karani, Charity Karimi, James Onyango Joel, crucial man Jeff Mwangemi, and Bill Odidi. Some of them are still employees at Broadcasting House.

We heard Leonard Mambo's voice every morning as we prepared to go to school, and on each of those mornings, he played the most annoying song I heard my whole childhood;

'Hata wewe mzee, amka kumekucha,
Kamata jembe na panga, uende shamba'

On Sundays, Billy Omala's school debate show started followed by Leonard Mambo's *'Jee, Huu ni Ungwana?'* before the lunchtime news. Those bulletins were long, from the minute you heard *'Rais Mtukufu* Daniel Toroitich Arap Moi all the way to when the last item on *Matangazo Maalum* and *Vifo',* almost an hour would be gone in one bulletin.

Something else also grabbed my attention—football. I don't remember the exact match the Harambee Stars was playing, but it was on a Saturday and we were in school for remedial lessons. One of the students had bumped into our deputy behind the boys' washrooms smoking, which was frowned upon especially if students were exposed to it.

To kill that vibe, the deputy went to the staffroom and gave us the school radio to listen to the live transmission of the match. Ali Salim Manga and Jack Oyoo Sylvester were in the booth, commentating that match so descriptively it was almost like we were at the stadium watching. That would be the first time I was hearing names like Reinhardt Fabisch (the only coach who took our national team to the greatest heights in as many years, and from rookies he had picked in the estates and high school competitions.) I remember we won that game by a goal to nil, but by the time the radio was being taken away, I knew Francis Onyiso, Musa Otieno, and Mike Cantona. Onyiso stood out, probably because the commentators spoke so highly of him, giving him a larger than life mental image that I carried home.

I made a personal commitment to know who this Onyiso was thus I started digging out information about Harambee Stars in newspapers and from radio. I told myself I was going to put faces behind those names at whatever cost. I started joining little gatherings where football was being discussed, and in not so long, I gathered when the next match was going to be played. It remains one of the most etched Harambee Stars matches in my mind. We were playing the Super Eagles from Nigeria at the Moi Sports Centre, Kasarani. Rumour had it that President Moi had promised the team cars if they won the match. As young a fan as I was, the wave was strong. I behaved my best that period, with the plan to sweet-talk Mom into letting me watch TV in the main house that afternoon. She agreed!

For the first time in my life, I sat and watched how a national team looked like. Harambee Stars was donned in black shorts and white tops with black stripes, 'KENYA' written on the front. Nigeria was in green shorts and green tops with a huge white stripe running from the neck downwards. An eagle was emblazoned at the front. Francis Onyiso was a slightly short, heavily built man with a bad temper. I added more names to my list: Ken Simiyu (who scored 'our' goal), John Baresi, John Luchuku, Mohammed Shariff, Tom Ogweno, and Erick Omondi. I saw Fabisch too, and to show just how serious this match was, President Moi himself was in the stadium. I also picked a few Nigerian names: Taribo West, Tijani Babangida, Celestine Babayaro, Uche Ukechukwu, Sunday Oliseh, Daniel Amokachi, and Jonathan Akpoborie—the man who equalized for the Eagles, forcing the match to end in a 1-1 draw.

Onyiso's command of goal and repeated scolding of his defenders made me discover what I was missing—being a goalkeeper. I had for so long shied away from being part of the footballing action in school since I was shunned for going to play with shoes, but the burning desire hit home. I was going back home, and this time I would be a goalkeeper, just like Onyiso so that I could jump around like a monkey and gather balls from opponents. Brooke Bond then went ahead to release tea packaging with passport photos of those players I had watched trouble Nigeria on TV. This football was quite something from the look of things!

I grew fonder of football, fond enough to know that as a Luhyia, I was an automatic AFC Leopards fanatic and an opponent of Gor Mahia. The rest like Kenya Breweries (now renamed Tusker), Shabana, Rivatex, or Ulinzi were just by-the-ways. It was AFC against Gor, period. Now I had two teams to look out for—AFC and Harambee Stars. The AFC goalkeeper was of course the first one I was interested in since that was now my area—Mathews Ottamax. Boy had antics in goal, and pride! Goalkeeping it was, no looking back.

'Project become goalkeeper' was launched and I hit the ground running. My first stop was joining the local football team to hone my 'skills'; skills I did not even have in the first place. We didn't have the bouncy leather ball like the one my role models played with; we had a homemade one woven out of plastic bags and thread, an excellent way of recycling plastic bags.

Every local team had one boy who was gifted in manufacturing the ball. Without him, there was no ball for the day, and whatever rules he made on the pitch stood. If he decided you were not being fielded that day no other teammate could overturn that, and when he got tired or protested a certain decision against his side he simply took his ball and went home. Game over. In most teams, the fattest boy was the automatic goalkeeper, maybe the notion was that his size would fill a bigger space at the goalpost, stopping more goals from getting in. I wasn't fat myself but there was an already 'fat' team goalkeeper at the team I chose to join, meaning for me to ever get anywhere near goal posts I had to remove him from the equation. That dude was good in goalkeeping, though, a mini-Onyiso, and seemed to have trained with the team for a while. He even went by the nickname Kanalelo, the towering goalkeeper of another team that had given Harambee Stars a run for its money. Moreover, the team couldn't just take up anyone from the streets and make them their goalkeeper. By the end of the day, I became the match ball boy.

Nevertheless, when disaster strikes, some benefit. Two weeks later, a team from the next village visited for a match. The chubby boy underperformed terribly in goalkeeping that day, he was such a disappointment to the team. We conceded almost eight goals, so the team captain decided to do damage control—he offered me the chance I had repeatedly begged for. No one had ever seen me in goal, but with their goalkeeper letting in goals like a sieve, they took a chance on me.

Though green in goalkeeping, I managed to save some, a little too many that I never thought I could. I conceded two, but that was a better record given whomever I had relieved duty from had let in four times that number. And just like that, I was the official number one! I was on cloud nine. The former goalkeeper was redeployed as a striker, and though he never scored a single goal all that time I was with the team, he seemed to enjoy the newfound position. I was happy, he was happy, the backline was compact; we became a revered team.

One Sunday, we had one of the most important matches; an away match, so far away that we had to walk a long distance to get there. I went missing from home soon after I left church and hooked up with the rest of the team. We got there slightly tired, but in a way, our muscles were warm enough to get right into the game. They had a worse playing ground than back home, and there was a pool of water near the goalpost that I kept sliding and landing into whenever I caught the ball. Other times, the ball would land in the puddle and splash water all over me. We lost the match by three goals to one, were rained on while going back home, and we arrived home late. Mom was already back home from her usual church missions, and though she seemed to have noticed my absence, she said nothing about it.

I slept a happy boy that night; one because I was gathering more field experience and the team seemed to have complete confidence in me even after the loss, and two because Mom was beginning to give me space and respect my decisions. Now, it was fair enough I needed to build on my experience, gain more confidence and rise through the ranks until Fabisch signed me up for Harambee Stars. I was intend on replacing Onyiso when the time came.

I woke up the next day with an unusual feeling. I was trembling so violently I couldn't even get out of bed. My teeth gnashed against each other and my body was covered in goose bumps. I remembered the previous day's episode and realised that perhaps I had pushed myself too hard or the rain had given me a hit. I forced my weak body out of bed, took breakfast, and walked to school. I had to be quick before *she* found out my sneaking the previous day had come home to roost. I suffered on that walk to school, struggled through the morning chores, and hardly managed to complete the first lesson.

When it was too much, I got out of class and went behind the boys' toilets to soak in the lazy morning sun. The trembling seemed to increase, and instead of feeling better I was shook from the core. At some point, I passed out and next I heard was the muzzled voice of Mr Lodenyo talking about staffroom and hospital. At some point, I managed to open my eyes and voila! Towering me, like a judge watchtower, was my mom!

She proposed we go home first, change out of my uniform, pick the hospital book then head to the Centre. We walked home silent, her stopping here and there as usual to have a tete-a-tete with her people. For a tyrant like her, that silence was so loud it made me uncomfortable. I was used to a mom who would drag me by the ear while beating and scolding me, so this new one was spooky. I told myself that maybe I was in such a bad shape she was worried I would collapse again. She at no point inquired what part of me was in pain or how I exactly felt, a question that always came out first whenever I felt sick.

I immediately went into my room to change while she went to gather all the other requirements from the main house. I was just turning around to go tell her I was ready for hospital when I walked straight into her, whip in hand. Let us just say I was whipped that morning, so much that I was so close to requesting for DNA testing to confirm I was not adopted.

It is now on this walk to hospital that she got back to the woman I knew. She scolded me all the way, said I went out to play football in the cold despite her continuous warnings to stay indoors. She also asked me to decide whether or not I was ready to continue schooling, if not, she asked that I stop wasting her money in the name of school fees. Even with all the love and dedication I had accorded goalkeeping, I had to make the painful decision of dropping all that investment. I was never going to play for that team again. It would be the first time in my life I had to let go and watch helplessly as my dream slipped out of my hands. Now you know why Harambee Stars has for the longest time struggled to get a dependable goalkeeper.

CHAPTER 13

A BRUSH WITH POWER

ONE BRIGHT MORNING, without warning nor prior preparation, a truck pulled into the school compound, reversed towards the staffroom, and offloaded brand new lockable desks. The head teacher walked towards the package looking confused, trying to wrap his mind around what was happening. A few teachers joined him, staring at those brand new desks in awe like the Bushmen of *The Gods Must Be Crazy* movie did with the coke bottle. They were still hovering around the desks when a 4X4 truck with huge speakers on the roof drove into the compound and came right up to the staffroom. Two men in sleek black suits and eyes concealed behind dark glasses stepped out and approached the teachers. All we did was peep through our classroom windows wondering what was happening.

The car and its occupants left immediately the bell rang.

"Nyumbaaani!" came the loud roar from the classrooms. We were accustomed to being sent home for fees or indefinite closings whenever the bell went at such a time. Everyone gathered at the assembly ground, one of the fastest ever convened. The rumourmongers had already cooked up the story that teachers were going on strike again because what they were promised when they last downed their tools was yet to be remitted. Teachers had a powerful union that time under one Ambrose Ayoyi who did not shy away from calling for strikes.

The headmaster stepped forward and with his croaking voice asked us to keep quiet. It was a bit difficult to control us when there were signs of going home. It was like the tie was strangling him, but poor son of a peasant had to keep it on the whole day lest the Teachers Service Commission sneaked into his office a letter relieving him of his duties.

"The girls will clean all the classes while the boys will pick litter from around the compound. Class seven and eight boys will carry all desks from upper primary classrooms and line them around the assembly. The prefects will supervise that assignment. Let work begin now!"

Cleaning? When did we ever start cleaning before being sent home? We were used to leaving the school as messed as it was then restoring order on opening. This was a bit off, but we obeyed. We were not sure whether to celebrate being out of class at an unusual time or get annoyed at the manual work that we all hated.

Things started unfolding slowly. First, a group of women dressed in the nearby Anglican Church choir uniform came into the school dancing and singing *'Mwanamberi'*, a song only accorded someone who has done something worth being proud of. To the best of our knowledge, we were a bunch of institutionalized brats being locked in the school to keep us out of trouble in the villages, so being the intended audience of that song was confusing. Next, the teachers came out of the staffroom dragging a folded tent, which they swiftly erected in a few minutes as we watched, shocked that our school owned one of those.

It is while we were still doing this clean up that the four-wheel-drive car came back and parked, then one of the two men started dishing out posters with the bust-up photo of a young man I did not know. The other one came out with a bag and out of it pulled *khangas* with the same writings as on the posters and gave one to each woman on the troupe. They broke into song again, a new one this time.

"Mundu achayanga Musalia witu, arakasambwe ni sitima!" (Whoever is looking down at our Musalia will be electrocuted!)

Now things started falling into place. The young man on the posters must be the Musalia the women were singing, and he must be so important for them to want an electrocution on anyone that dared touch him. I think I wanted to be that young man then, forget Onyiso, so that women would leave their chores, put on uniform and dance around singing m name. I wanted to be him so that whenever my posters were distributed, school programs stopped and students were asked to go clean their school compound, including their teachers. Now I was sure the new desks must have come from him. This young man was generous; buying desks for our school, printing posters, and now giving *khangas* to women! But he must also be rich; I wasn't exactly good at Math but could tell all this had cost a tidy sum.

The bell rang again and we assembled, at least aware that we were not going home as expected and a young rich man was being praised in song for giving us desks and clothing church women.

"Mbunge wetu, Mheshimiwa Musalia Mudavadi anatutembelea leo. Kwa hivyo kila mmoja wenu awe na tabia nzuri hadi sherehe hiyo ikalimilike. Si mnaona ametuletea desk *mpya?"*

One of the women burst into another song, followed by the rest of the group:

Kukubiri ichama amakono (Lets clap for our party!)
Kukubiri ichama amakonoo (Lets clap for our party!)

They sang and danced for a few minutes then went quiet. Directions were given on our standing arrangements before we were told to go to the playground and wait for the next piece of information. Everyone got into break time mood as usual; girls on one side skipping rope and singing *'by shot I love you baby'* and boys on the other playing football. At some point, the excitement died as hunger and thirst started kicking in, even the once vibrant women sat under a tree shade. The students who loved to sneak sneaked, those that were fond of fighting fought, and those of us who always got hungry started yawning all over the place.

Lunchtime came and went, we still held on, waiting for that piece of information we had been promised. The information came as a motorcade of about fifteen vehicles, mostly sleek black sedans. One of the vehicles, a green one written Land Rover Discovery flew the Kenyan flag and had two men on both sides running after it. The doors flung open and out stepped a sharply dressed young man with a huge smile. That was the same guy I had seen on the posters! Wow! I had not seen someone look that sharp and kempt. That was even the first time I was seeing this monster brand of car called 'Discovery' despite being the one on the hunt for car models.

There were three policemen hovering around the 'Discovery'. It looked elegant enough to be the car of choice for someone as important and respected as him. I admired the huge wheels, the spare one perched at the rear, the bull bars at the front, clear lights and the flag being blown leisurely by the afternoon breeze.

Our school was no longer a centre for organization and discipline, it was a stampede zone with villagers squeezing and haranguing each other to catch a glimpse of the goings on at the front. The women sung their hearts out, like their whole lives depended on it. I at some point saw the young man approach them holding a white envelope. They let him into the little circle they had formed, where he danced too, badly, like the worst dance I had ever seen before he handed one of the women the envelope then went back to his seat. He was sent off with one giant ululation.

After a while, he stood up to speak into some two microphones passed across by one of the black-suited men. When he spoke, his voice was heard in the horn speakers on top of the 4X4D vehicle.

All I heard from that young man was *"Bla bla kura bla KANU bla ble si mnajua bla ble."* The only complete sentence I got was *"Hizo* desk *nimeleta zisaidie wanafunzi wetu."* The teachers clapped, the women ululated, and we simply watched, our minds concerned about our grumbling stomachs. Immediately the young man finished talking, he was yanked into the Discovery and the motorcade disappeared as quickly as it had come.

In 1997, Tope was in his last year of primary school education. All pupils doing the Kenya Certificate for Primary Education (KCPE) were referred to as candidates. As the trend was, success cards were sent from friends and relatives through the school post box then they were read out on assembly every evening. It was therefore possible to know who had received the most success wishing cards, and who was yet to be remembered as a candidate by their folks. Candidates looked forward to that moment given that some success cards came with a fifty or hundred shillings note enclosed, a motivation that uplifted you financially at the snap of a finger. They had images of different couples with different poses and smiles on the cover, then a message inside the card. The sophisticated ones had these gadgets affixed at the centre that let out soothing melodies the moment you opened the card. Now, picture a class of about ten each with their melodious cards open—it was a cacophony of ear-piercing electronic screams.

Our education system was in a way that KCPE had an almost fifty percent stake in how your future would pan out. You failed to do well in the exams and your career path was as good as sealed, reason most boys in Column 3 are now confined to ferrying passengers on motorbikes for a living. There were seven examinable papers spread across three days, Tuesday to Thursday, with Monday being the preparation day when the candidates scrubbed their desks clean of any markings and writings on them and purchased Kofa or Oxford geometrical sets and clipboards. Parents treated you much better these few days, trying to rally behind you so that you didn't deliver embarrassing results which were usually posted on the open noticeboard for the whole village to see. Teachers popped in here and there to offer their last minute advice and revision papers, aware that in that bunch lay the image the school would carry the following year. If pupils did well then parents would be proud of the school, which meant more students, and a loophole for the school administration to sneak in little unwarranted fees here and there without raising questions. Being a candidate was the best feeling in the world then, especially if you were one who was sure KCPE would be an avenue for you to shine and appear on top of the list that would be hung when results were released.

Tope received two melody success wishing cards from the twins who were now in high school. We celebrated the feat. Thatcher, in her mysterious ways, got wind of those cards. She did not only sneak into our room and steal them but also showed up at school with them the following day.

Tope had not even noticed that the cards were missing from his bag until we were called to the staffroom and saw them spread on the teachers' desk. She had already explained to the teachers that Miriam and Keith were our neighbours who had no reason whatsoever to send Tope expensive cards unless we had something going on that they had to investigate. The staffroom was divided into two; half the teachers seeing nothing wrong with receiving cards from neighbours when you are sitting for an exam. Again, how do you start putting a whole candidate through a rigorous investigation just a few days to his exam? If he performed poorly he would easily use that as the scapegoat and be believed, then the same teachers would be on the chopping board for traumatizing a student to failure. The other half, the trigger-happy, and every school has these, agreed with Mom that this was a matter worth an investigation.

While they were still haggling over whether this was legal or illegal, Tope and I made faces at each other as we did when it was time to lock our evidence and play victims. We could not have kept a strong pact all those years to let it go at this time. Our affair with those girls, though not sexual, had survived Mom's scrutiny for so long the bubble was not going to burst that easily. We gave the narrative that they were just harmless friends and it was them reading malice where there wasn't. The innocence narrative seemed to win over even those that had insisted we be investigated, and soon it was agreed that we be allowed to go back to our classrooms as they 'looked into it further.' They retained the cards, with reason that they were distracting Tope from concentrating on the approaching exam. We have never seen them since; I think Tope is still preparing for KCPE.

CHAPTER 14

TWILIGHT YEARS

THE YEAR 1998 brought the most difficult changes in my life, one that opened my eyes to a different kind of world. First, Tope had performed well in KCPE and had been called to a provincial boy's boarding school far from home, taking with him a part of my heart. For seven years, he had woken up with me, walked with me to and from school, gotten into mischief with me, and gotten punished alongside me. His mistakes had been mine, where he went I went, his friends had been my friends, now all that was gone with the wind— like it never existed in the first place. To add salt to injury, our twins (who were in a mixed school) met other boys and forgot about us. In any case, I was now alone and still couldn't tell them apart, how would I have managed?

I was a candidate. I took too long to adapt to the new changes and what it meant to be a candidate. Mom was at my neck, that I was taking this year a bit too casually, forgetting Tope had set five hundred plus points in KCPE as the yardstick for me. She hardly saw me sit on the study table revising, I never asked her to bring me past papers from her school, and I was sluggish in the mornings. I was crumbling inside, and it got worse seeing the twins in the morning in the company of other boys. Sometimes parents hardly take time to understand the battles their kids are going through but not saying, or wanting to but not knowing how to. Moreover, it was difficult to open up to Mom.

My speed dial imaginary friend, the bad angel, was to my aid more often than not. *You are now a badass man you need badass company,* he whispered. I started attending Disco *Matanga*—night entertainment offered to bereaved families and friends. People dance to music and song through the night to the break of the day to keep the household alive. It would be a sad funeral if every night only the family and relatives sat there with the body of their loved one with no one else to share their pain.

I was good at being mischievous. I rose through the ranks of being an attendee and dancer to being the DJ at all Disco *Matangas* in the village. This notwithstanding, I was a candidate and expected is to spend my valuable time studying, but that gave me some sort of escape from the realities of my disintegrating life. Those days, audiotapes and vinyl were the thing.

The audiotapes came with Side A and B, and what we know as albums nowadays were called 'Volumes'. Every deejay needed a Bic biro pen and someone to help rewind or fast-forward the next tape in line while he selected the music. Skipping or repeating a song meant rewinding or forwarding through another whole song before getting to the intended one, and you were not sure you would find it at the exact beginning.

Piracy did not start the other day. We called it dubbing. All you needed was the source tape, a blank C60, C90, or C120 tape and a system with two decks, one of which had a red record button. The tapes would be mounted on the decks, the blank one being on the record deck then the source in the other. Precision would be required to press the play button on the source tape and record button on the blank tape at the same time. You would then wait and watch through the deck window as the two tapes rolled on, creating an exact replica of the source tape. You just had to pray that none of them stopped or malfunctioned for whatever reason; otherwise, you would have to repeat the process from top.

After dubbing both side A and B, there would be the moment of anxiety as you did a trial playing session on the receiving tape to confirm all the songs had been dubbed. Other times the 'blank' tape would not be new but one with previous material so you were overwriting it. Most of them were stolen from friends or parents, dubbed on and made to look totally different from the original even if it meant painting them. The downside with this was that the original recording on the tape would keep popping up on the new material so you would have distorted music. My dad had these four albums he held dear: *Malebo* by Munishi, TP OK Jazz, Kenny Rogers, and Bonnie M which went missing from his collection and joined mine, now rebranded as Ntombi, Girlie Mafura, UB40, and Bob Marley.

I got to know about King Lion Sounds from a mix tape someone pushed my way at a DJ jig and suggested I play it. It gave me a chance to listen to more artists and songs amidst the noise by Papa Charlie and his crew. You could tell by listening to the mix tape that wherever it was recorded rocked. I invested so much time in getting to know more about Reggae, artists and the messages in their songs that I started being consulted about latest releases and history of reggae artists.

Disco *Matanga* paid back handsomely. I had been invited to deejay at a funeral in the neighbourhood; a routine that took away most of my nights. As I was busy selecting music and lining it up, some soft palm touched my hand. I turned to see a beautiful girl placing a cup of tea next to my deck. I scrutinized her, all the way to the face, and right there I knew I had found a perfect replacement for my lost twin. I watched her hand slide in front of me, put the cup down on the table, and shimmer away. Good thing with being a DJ is that you have an edge over everyone else dancing in the crowd, so when I requested her to come join my booth after delivering tea to everyone, she agreed. And Frozine became my new girlfriend.

It also remains the one funeral that exposed me to Dad whom I had not seen for long. He happened to be visiting from the city when the burial was being held. He was fond of travelling at night so we would wake up in the morning and, *voila,* he was at the breakfast table. This occasion was no different—when I was busy wooing my new catch in the dead of the night, he was on his way home. The image I had of Dad since I was a baby was of a serious guy who only watched as others goofed around. He smiled only when there was need to, and participated if whatever he was to say looked and felt like wisdom. He was like a royal. It is his stiffness that even made most of us, his children, not go out full force at events and share in the fun, we adopted his rat-in-a-corner style.

As it was and still is the norm when there's a burial, the whole family attended. Dad kept his usual composure. Like any other burial where I come from, there comes a session when the mourners congregate around the grave, sing and dance in circles as the grave is being filled up. It is usually the final respect to the departed. This time no one does dirges;

just normal songs of celebration to show the departed that they had ran and won the race.

My eyes caught someone who wasn't expected to be part of that dancing troupe—Dad. In his well-cut suit, trimmed hair and well-polished shoes, he was dancing so vigorously that many stopped looking at everyone else and focused on him. I stood in awe and watched as my usually serious Dad twitched and shook his broad shoulders to the melody like nothing in the world mattered. It was like he was on steroids. At that time, I was almost convinced my old man had smoked a joint. And he did not seem to tire; he gave the well-drilled professional funeral dancers a run for their money. The drummers had to beat their drums more intensely to be in tandem with his moves, sending him into more frenzy. People would tap my shoulder from behind and point at him to show me in case I had not noticed. I just nodded. When the drums fell silent, he went back to his composed self and has never done that again.

CHAPTER 15

DRUNK

A MAN CAN forget so many things, but he never forgets the times he saw his mother cry, especially if it was him that made her shed tears. As annoyed as she always made you, as bad a mother you thought she was, a mother's tears cut through your heart like a sharp razor. I have such a moment in my life. Yes, I made Thatcher, the same macho woman who brought me up with an iron fist, cry; cold sad tears.

That same evening after the funeral in which my old man stole the show, the new boy living next door came to my house and asked me to accompany him, which I innocently did. Turns out his intentions were to introduce me to his girlfriend who was visiting. Like any other young man would do in support of a friend, I crossed over from our compound through a tiny gate between the two compounds and went to his house. He had not even completed the introductions when Dad walked in and found my hand extended to reach hers. Why he was there, no one knows. Whatever made him follow me is a question I have never bothered to ask.

He led me back home with kicks even as I struggled to plead my innocence. He had this construed notion that the girl he had just seen was mine, hidden at my neighbours' until everyone went to sleep then I would sneak her into my house. I had not even gotten that girl's name, but who would listen and believe? Not Dad. The man who had put aside all his worries in life earlier in the day and loosened up before the whole multitude of mourners was now scolding me so violently over a girl I had just met that evening. Was he even aware my latest relationship with Frozine was hardly twenty-four hours old?

Ever been crucified by both parents over a false allegation? That breaks someone's heart in a big way. So, Dad would say whatever he had on one side, then Mom would join and say hers and the cycle continued. Sometimes they would talk at the same time, leaving me wondering who to listen to now that every word was meant for me. I held myself back so much that day. The scolding was so intense that grandma, who was now living with us, joined in and told my parents to stop talking. If anything, they were too loud and making it impossible for her to sleep.

She asked me to accompany her to her room where she started telling me stories from her past. Her hands looked frail and most of the flesh had sunk, leaving the outline of her bones almost popping out. Her skin was pale, lips peeled and most of her hair had fallen off leaving only a few grey strands. She didn't even know when exactly she was born, so her age was always estimated. She always forgot my name, but on this night she remembered, plus many other details about me, like the fact that I had mentioned choosing Nyang'ori High School as one of my preferred schools for secondary.

"There's this bushy compound opposite Nyang'ori. Your late grandfather worked for a white man who lived there."

The compound she was talking about is currently occupied by Shakeel Shabir, one of the well-known politicians in Kisumu.

"I would go visit him so many times when I felt lonely, and soon became good friends with the white man's wife. She even nicknamed me Mamisaf."

She let out her usual laughter.

"That white woman loved fish. Every Monday and Thursday she would send me to Kiboswa to bring fish for the family. All those women who smoked fish in Kiboswa knew me by name," she added.

"Every time I went there they would be like 'Jeliha come and get fish for your white man from here'," she laughed, her hand shaking.

"Whenever schools were almost closing, your grandfather would give me some pennies and send me back home to go wait for the children. Your father who was my last born was notorious for not wanting to go back to school so I had to keep pushing him on opening day."

She went quiet at this point, like she was trying to refresh her memory, or probably giving me time to ponder over the fact that my dad was truant in his childhood.

"Would you believe that white woman's boat capsized one day when she was sailing on the lake?"

A sad look fell upon her face, followed by a prolonged silence. I noticed she was trying to suppress tears. It had been over fifty years since she lost her white friend, but you could tell the grief had never completely left her. She cleared her throat.

"It is after that tragedy that the white man decided it was time to go back to Europe. Your grandfather had to come back home and do farming."

She started humming to herself then slid back into her blanket. I knew she had already forgotten I was by her bedside listening to her stories. I switched off her light and walked back to my bedroom.

That session with grandma was a good escape from the anger I was carrying after that wrongful scolding. Justice in our household had become elusive for so many years; it was like no one was ever innocent. I went to bed burning inside, wondering why no one ever gave me the benefit of doubt. I had been victimized at school, by girlfriends, the justice system at home, and everyone else around me.

The bad angel never let a moment pass him. As I was turning in my bed trying to force sleep, I heard a knock on my window—two of my Disco *Matanga* boys were here. They mentioned that Impact Sounds had a show at North-End Bar in Mbale, so all we needed was to grab some drinks then go dance the night away at that disco. That was a lucrative proposition considering the mental state I was in; I was game even before they finished breaking down the nitty-gritties.

I threw a jacket over what I was wearing and led them out. The idea was to get Jik, concentrated *chang'aa* that knocked you out faster than your brain could know what was happening. Despite my mischief, this would be my first time drinking alcohol. We went to Rama's, grabbed our Jik then went to one of their houses to drink, get high then go for disco already inebriated.

I woke up the following day a few minutes past nine. My head felt like a stone. It quickly hit me that the bunch of keys in my pockets held a key to almost every other house in that compound, apart from the main house. That I had the key meant for the cowshed meant the cows had not been milked that day; breakfast, which depended on milk from those same cows had not been prepared and grandma had stayed locked indoors up to that point.

I staggered home.

By the time I got there, no one was talking to me. Mom just asked for the keys. Dad was missing, and I was to learn that he had gone to look for me at the police station. He was so sure I had gotten arrested the previous night. The hangover was killing me, so I headed straight to bed and blacked out again.

I woke up to find Mom seated beside my bed, tears rolling down her cheeks, looking at a once promising son and bright student disintegrating under her very eyes. Her only son, her first born, was now not just getting into mischief and hiding girls in people's houses but also drinking himself into a stupor. The respected teacher who had for years guided children from other families to success was now watching her own stray off course, and he had to just wait to become a candidate to do this. The final exam was a few months away, and here was the star that everyone looked up to in bits and pieces, with a swollen upper lip and a cracked lower one. Even in my drunken state, I could tell my actions had hurt her deeply. I was so pained I told myself I was not going to touch *chang'aa* again.

When that school term ended, I had dropped to position 3, a position I had not held since lower primary. Things were thick. Even I felt the pinch, enough to jolt me out of that slumber and focus back on books.

CHAPTER 16

FLY AWAY, BUTTERFLY

THAT HOLIDAY, TOPE came over to visit with stories of bullying in high school, bad food, manoeuvring Form One, and things I had not seen at our school like Science Laboratories and Engineering Workshops. He also had another piece of information—during one of their school outings, he had met and wooed a beautiful girl from another school. Her name was Maureen. The even better news was that Maureen was from around so she would be visiting that weekend to say hi to us. I shared my escapades too, including my new girlfriend.

Maureen visited. She walked through the gate into our compound with her head high, her light complexion lighting the way where her wedges stepped on. She was in a polka dot dress and had long lustrous hair and a finesse I hadn't seen in all the girls I had met. Tope was all smiles. When she smiled back, she expose a slit of snow-white teeth. I was taken in by hr beauty, the famous Maureen; Tope had gotten himself a smashing hot woman.

"Tope! *Huyu ni nani,*" Thatcher's voice boomed across the compound.

"Maureen," he replied.

"Maureen *ni nani kwako?*"

"Girlfriend."

"Heeeeeeh! Umeenda Form One *ukaona umeshakuwa mzee sana kuwa na* girlfriend, *eeh?"*

Maureen stood there dumbfounded while Tope and I remained quiet. Mom tore into that newfound love; spoke, and spoke, and spoke; all that time Maureen just watch, not sure what to do.

For all the drama in the world, Frozine walked in, sent by her people to bring some information from the just concluded funeral for Mom to add to the church data.

"Frozine!" Mom shouted.

"Wewe pia mambo yako na Hillary *staki! Ungoje umalize shule, Hillary pia amalize shule, mkitaka kuoana mimi sina shida! Unaskia?"*

Frozine stopped in her tracks.

"Mimi staki kulea watoto wa watoto saa hii!" Mom continued.

Frozine was quiet. She was collateral damage in a war she was not part of. I was too heartbroken to hear the rest of what Mom said, my heart bled for her.

"Nisiwahi kuona na Hillary *tena! Staki mchezo yenu."*

I have never forgotten the humbled image of Frozine walking away from our compound, and subsequently out of my life.

EPILOGUE

I SAT DOWN and looked through my life as a young boy growing in the village under a mother who was a teacher. In doing so, three things presented: first, I missed a huge aspect of paternal upbringing, something that still recurs in many households to date. I do not blame my old man, though, because he had to be away in order for our family to have the comfortable life we had. It was a difficult balance, and although he fell short of one or two areas expected of him as a father, he did what he had to do. We have been trying to mend that bond and make up for lost time. Sometimes I feel like we should have done this earlier.

Second, I was lucky to have the privilege to put on the only pair of shoes in the whole school, because it opened my eyes to the antagonism between the rich and poor at a tender age, a lesson that has informed how I look at life. Asked to describe my shoes in three words, I would call them 'a necessary evil'. Evil in the sense that they represent the hate and envy mankind attracts from would-be friends when they cannot keep up with his or her progress. They were not just shoes, they protected me on one part and exposed me to trouble on the other.

The third this is that women are powerful beings. That Mom was running a household alone, went to work every day, and still kept us in check required a lot of energy. A man would struggle a bit in the same position while trying so hard to hang onto sanity. This book therefore celebrates womanhood in entirety, only that the best words to describe it all lack.

ABOUT THE AUTHOR

Hillary Lisimba Ambani is an avid reader and writer. He studied Journalism and Mass Communication at the University of Nairobi. He has worked as a producer at Kenya Broadcasting Corporation and Flave Media in Tanzania. *The Boy with Shoes* is his first in a series of five books that revolve around the intricacies of what it means to be in a country that is always almost taking off but never does.